Christr...

The African boy listened carefully as the teacher explained why it is that Christians give presents to each other on Christmas day. "The gift is an expression of our joy over the birth of Jesus and our friendship for each other," she said.

When Christmas day came, the boy brought the teacher a sea shell of lustrous beauty. "Where did you ever find such a beautiful shell?" the teacher asked.

The youth told her that there was only one spot where such extraordinary shells could be found—a certain bay several miles away.

"Why . . . why, it's gorgeous," said the teacher. "But you shouldn't have gone all that way to get a gift for me."

His eyes brightening, the boy answered, "Long walk part of gift."

—from *The Guideposts Christmas Treasury*

Guideposts Treasuries from Bantam Books
Ask your bookseller for the books you have missed

The Guideposts Christmas Treasury

BANTAM BOOKS
TORONTO · NEW YORK · LONDON · SYDNEY

THE GUIDEPOSTS CHRISTMAS TREASURY

*A Bantam Book / published by arrangement with
Doubleday & Company, Inc.*

PRINTING HISTORY

*The Guideposts Christmas Treasury was originally published
by Guideposts Associates in 1972.
Doubleday edition published September 1980
Bantam edition / November 1981*

Bantam Books are published by Bantam Books, Inc. Its trademark, consisting of the words ''Bantam Books'' and the portrayal of a rooster, is Registered in U.S. Patent and Trademark Office and in other countries. Marca Registrada. Bantam Books, Inc., 666 fifth Avenue, New York, New York 10103.

PRINTED IN THE UNITED STATES OF AMERICA

0 9 8 7 6 5 4 3 2 1

Introduction

The acceptance of our first "treasury" encouraged us to proceed with another idea we had been harboring in our minds for several years—the dream of bringing together a collection of the best Christmas features from the pages of Guideposts. Finally, we decided to do just that and thus we began work on *The Guideposts Christmas Treasury* which you now hold in your hands. It was a long and difficult task—selecting the best of the best, but we feel it was worth it.

This volume, we believe, may very well be the most inspirational Christmas book of its kind ever published. Never before to our knowledge has a single book brought together so many outstanding Christmas articles, poems and short features. Many stories included have become classics—reprinted and retold again and again. Other newer works may in time gain classic status.

In the Guideposts tradition, we have selected material written by or about people from all walks of life. As you will see, some of the writers are world famous; other bylines are little known. Some of the stories are beautifully written; others derive their beauty from an honest simplicity.

To gather this material the editors have drawn from material which has (1) either appeared in the magazine since 1945 or (2) been published in our annual eight-page Christmas greeting booklet, first made available in 1953 and now printed in the millions each year. Regardless of its source there is one thing every story has in common: it has that special "heart" ingredient which can break down the walls that divide men and replace them with bridges of love and understanding.

We have divided our Christmas Treasury into ten categories. The stories in each section are punctuated with the most outstanding illustrations we have presented over the years. They have been produced by some of the country's top artists. Also, at random, we have included many favorite poems and short stories—all with a point to ponder, all full of some insight or truth about Christmas. In total, there are more than 100 features.

These stories are our favorites; we hope they are or do in fact become some of your favorites, too. We also hope that this book stirs in you anew the real Spirit of Christmas, the Spirit that led God to send His only Son to earth, the Spirit that brought the Wise Men bearing gifts, the Spirit that humbles, warms, uplifts, inspires and ennobles all who open their heart to it. May your heart be filled with that Spirit this season as never before. Merry Christmas.

The Editors

Contents

Section III
Christmas—A Time for Patience

Section IV
Christmas—A Time for Giving

Section V
Christmas—A Time for Understanding

Section VI
Christmas—A Time for Children

Section VII
Christmas—A Time for Learning

Section VIII
Christmas—A Time for Sharing

Section IX
Christmas—A Time for Love

Section X
Christmas—A Time for Remembering

Time for Christmas

Christmas is a time of anticipation,
When hope becomes a shining star,
When children's wishes become prayers,
And days are X'ed on calendar.

Christmas is a time for healing,
When disagreers and disagreements meet,
When long-time wounds are mended
And love moves hatred to retreat.

Christmas is a time for patience,
When we try anew to mold
Our lives in the image of Him
Whose birthday we uphold.

Christmas is a time for giving,
The Wise Men brought their best,
But Christ showed that the gift of self
Will out-give all the rest.

Christmas is a time for understanding
People and customs throughout the world,
When for all-too-brief a season,
The banner of peace is unfurled.

Christmas is a time for children
No matter what their age,
Spirit is the only ticket,
And heart the only gauge.

Christmas is a time for learning
A time when new truths unfold,
And not-so-innocent children
Often teach the old.

Christmas is a time for sharing,
A time for needy hands to clasp,
A time for stretching out in faith
With a reach that exceeds our grasp.

Christmas is a time for love,
A time for inhibitions to shed,
A time for showing that we care,
A time for words too long unsaid.

Christmas is a time to remember
Timeless stories from days of yore,
A time to ponder what's ahead,
A time to open another door.

Fred Bauer

The Guideposts Christmas Treasury

Section I
Christmas—A Time of Anticipation

Christmas is a time of anticipation,
When hope becomes a shining star,
When children's wishes become prayers,
And days are X'ed on calendar.

One of America's most talented
writers shares a Christmas classic.

The Night the Stars Sang
by Dorothy Canfield Fisher

At odd, quiet hours in her day, almost every mother wonders about her child's immortal soul. When will it emerge from the little ragamuffin who has just left his wet lollipop on the davenport? When will the person inside come to the surface? Will anyone be there to see, and to wonder?

I know a mother who was there, who did see and who did wonder. She told me about it, and I don't think she will mind if I tell you. It all began a few weeks before Christmas...

"Well," she said cheerily one afternoon to David, her eight-year-old and two of his friends, "what Christmas songs are you learning in your classroom this year?"

Looking down at his feet, David answered sadly, "Teacher says we can't sing good enough. She's only going to let kids sing in the entertainment who carry a tune."

Inwardly the mother broke into a mother's rage at a teacher. "So that's what she says, does she? What's she for, if not to teach children what they don't know?"

She drew in a deep breath, then said quietly, "Well, how'd you like to practice your song with me?"

Together the four went into the living room to the piano. "What song is your class to sing?"

"It came upon the midnight—" said the three boys, speaking at once.

"That's a nice one," she commented, reaching for the battered songbook on top of the piano. "This is the way it goes." She played the air and sang the first two lines.

They opened their mouths and sang out lustily:

"It came upon the midnight
    clear
That glorious song of old..."

3

At the end of that phrase, David's mother stopped abruptly, and for an instant bowed her head over the keys. Her feeling about Teacher made a right-about turn.

She finally lifted her head, turned a smiling face on the three waiting children. "I tell you what," she said, "the way, really, to learn a tune is just one note after another. I'll strike just the two first notes on the piano—It came—" Full of good will the little boys sang with her.

She stopped. Breathed hard.

"Not quite," she said, with a false smile, "Pre-t-ty good. I think we'd better take it one note at a time. Bill, you try it."

After a pause . . . "Peter—it's your turn."

That evening, after the children had gone to bed, she told her husband, "You never heard anything like that in your whole life, Harry. Never. You can't imagine what it was like!"

"Oh, yes I can too," he said over his temporarily lowered newspaper. "I've heard plenty of tone deaf-kids hollering. I know what they sound like. There are people, you know, who really can't carry a tune."

Seeing, perhaps, in her face, the mulish mother-stubbornness, he added, with a little exasperation, "What's the use of trying to do what you can't do?"

That was reasonable, she thought. But the next morning, when she was downtown doing her marketing, she turned in at the public library and picked up two books on teaching music to children.

During the weeks between then and the Christmas entertainment, the mother didn't see how she could ever keep it up. She discovered to her dismay that the little boys had no idea whether a note was higher or lower than the one before it.

She adapted and invented "musical games" to train their ear for this. Standing in a row, their backs to the piano, listening whether the second note was "up hill or down hill" from the first note, the boys thought it as good a game as any other. They laughed raucously over each other's mistakes, ran a contest to see who came out best.

There were times when the mother faltered. Many times. When she saw the ironing heaped high, or when her daughter, Janey, was in bed with a cold, she would say to herself, "Now today I'll just tell the boys that I cannot go on with this. We're not getting anywhere, anyhow."

Then she would remember that Christmas celebrated the birth of the Savior—and that one of Christ's most beloved traits was patience.

So when the boys came storming in, certain that she would not close that door she had half-opened for them, she laid everything aside and went to the piano.

As a matter of fact, they were getting somewhere. Even with their backs to the piano, the boys could now tell, infallibly, whether a second note was above or below the first one. Along about the second week of December, they could all sound—if they remembered to sing softly and to listen to themselves—a note, any note, within their range, she struck on the piano.

After that it went fast; the practicing of the song, repeating it for the at first skeptical and then thoroughly astonished teacher, and then their triumphant report at home, "Teacher says we can sing it good enough. She says we can sing with the others. We practiced going up on the platform this afternoon."

Then the day of the Christmas entertainment: boys clumping up the aisle, the girls switching their short skirts proudly. David's mother clutched her handbag nervously.

The crash from the piano giving them the tone, all the mouths open,

"It came upo-on the midnight
    clear
That glorious so-ong of old . . ."

The mother's tense hands relaxed. Teacher's long drill and hers had been successful. It was not howling, it was singing. There were swelling crescendos and at the lines:

"The world in so-olemn stillness
    lay
To hear the a-angels sing . . ."

the child voices were hushed in a diminuendo. Part of the mother's very life, she thought wryly, had been spent in securing her part of the diminuendo.

So there he stood, her little David, a fully accredited part of his corner of society, as good as anybody, the threat of the inferiority feeling averted this time. The door had been slammed in his face. She had pushed it open, and he had gone through.

The hymn ended. The burst of parental applause began clamorously. The third grade filed down from the platform.

Surely, now, the mother thought, David would turn his head to where she sat and thank her with a look. Just this once.

He did turn his head as he filed by. He looked full at his family, at his father, his mother, his kid sister, his big brother and his sister from the high school. He gave them a formal, small nod to acknowledge publicly that they were his family. But his mother knew that his look was not for her alone. It was just as much for those of his family who had been bored and impatient spectators of her struggle to help him, as for her who had given part of her life to roll that stone uphill.

She sighed. Mothers were to accept what they received, without bitterness, without resentment. After all, that was what mothers worked for—not for thanks, but to do their job. The sharp chisel of life, driven home by experience, flanked off expertly another flint-hard chip from her blithe, selfish girlhood. It fell away from the woman she was growing to be, and dropped soundlessly into the abyss of time . . .

But a few nights later, close to Christmas, the mother looked out her kitchen window to see if David was returning from a neighbor's. The night was cloudless, cold and still. Her backyard was almost transparent in the pale radiance that fell from the stars.

Then she saw David. Knee-deep in the snow he stood, looking all around him. Then he lifted his face towards the sky. What could he be looking at? Or hearing?

She opened the kitchen door and stepped out into the dark, under the stars. He came quickly to her, and put his arms around her. With every fiber of her body which had borne his, she felt a difference in him.

"It's so still," he said quietly in a hushed voice, a voice she had never heard before.

"All those stars," he murmured dreamily, "they shine so. But they don't make a sound."

He stood a little away from her to look up into her face. "Do you remember—in the song—'the world in solemn stillness lay'?"

The starlight showed him clear, his honest, little-boy eyes wide, fixed trustingly on his mother's, and in them she saw the miracle—the miracle of an awakening soul.

He had not known that he had an inner sanctuary. Now he

stood in it, awe-struck at his first sight of beauty, and opened the door to his mother.

As naturally, as he breathed, he put into her hands the pure rounded pearl of a shared joy.

"I thought I heard them singing—sort of," he whispered.

Let Christmas Happen to You
by Norman Vincent Peale

Christmas is a season of joy and laughter when our cup of happiness brims over. Yet increasingly we hear negative remarks about what a burden the holiday season has become.

This indicates that something is wrong somewhere because Christ never meant His birthday to be anything but a glorious event. Christianity is designed for the transmission of power from Jesus Christ to the individual; a Christ-centered Christmas, therefore, should be the year's climactic experience.

Perhaps we need to use more imagination in recapturing this experience in a personal way, like some creative people are doing.

For example, in front of a Texas gasoline station there hung a big sign last December which read: "Merry Christmas and a Happy New Year to all my customers. The $150 that would be spent on your Christmas cards has gone to help the Rev. Bill Harrod bring Christmas cheer to West Dallas."

In another section of the country a church congregation was asked to bring in all the old clothes they could spare for distribution to the needy. One family sent in all new clothes, bought with money diligently saved all year to buy each other Christmas presents.

Such giving surely expresses the true meaning of the birthday of Our Lord. We best honor Him when we live the examples He set. An act of mercy that reflects the inspiration He gave us will create a deeper satisfaction and happiness than giving or receiving the most expensive gift.

Ten years ago the daughter of Mr. and Mrs. Carl Hansen of San Bernardino, California, died of cancer. She was seven years old. After time had healed some of their grief the Hansens realized their little daughter had taught them so much about a child's love that they wished to perpetuate what she had given them. They decided that Mr. Hansen would dress as Santa Claus and together they would visit every bedridden child in town who could not see Santa in the stores.

In two years they were so busy each Christmas that the Elks supplied a gift for each child they visited. Mr. Hansen learned magic to entertain the children, then collected amateur entertainers and developed a show for each visit. There were so many homes and hospitals with love-hungry children that the Hansens eventually decided to make their Christmas visiting a year-round project.

The Psalmist says: "I will remember the works of the Lord: surely I will remember thy wonders of old." The early Christians celebrated Christmas by remembering the works of the Lord and the wonders of old. It was a day for gaiety, but not for excess. There is something blasphemous and pagan about using the birthday of Jesus as an excuse for exaggerated and commercialized giving and heavy drinking. How many people do we all know who make gift-giving a burden because they spend beyond their means? In their effort to keep up with the Joneses many actually go into debt. They would better express the spirit of Christmas if their gift had more understanding in it than money. Here is an example of what I mean:

In Hewlett, Long Island, the Jewish residents formed a congregation, but did not have a temple, and met in a store. The membership outgrew the store, and right before the Christmas holiday they started a building drive for a temple. One of their neighbors, a Roman Catholic named Ricky Cardance, turned over his filling station to his Jewish friends on Christmas and New Year's Day. They would operate it, and all the receipts would go into their building fund.

So giving at Christmas can take many forms not measured by dollars. Here are a few simple suggestions for such giving:

A gift you make yourself is more appreciated—something as simple as a fruit cake or a letter opener; a surprise photo of someone's house, babies or pets. A couple we know painted the porch and front door of their parents' house. To the giver it is a labor of love; to the receiver an offering of love.

The members of one family, during a financial crisis, made

personally, by hand, all gifts for each other. This particular Christmas was such a joyful one that its plan has been continued ever since.

If you know of a mother who would like to go out to church, or other activities, but cannot afford a baby sitter, why not give her a gift certificate for a dozen hours of babysitting for the year to come?

Send Christmas remembrances to those who would least expect it from you; the people we often encounter but do not really know: the neighbor who nods good morning daily; the people who clean your office or workroom; the officer who directs traffic at your corner. Best of all, the person you've been most annoyed with!

Making it a point to find out more about these people is an enriching experience. Get the thrill of trips to a hospital, orphanage, a jail. Also it is a wonderful Christmas adventure to help the families of such unfortunates.

Often it is left to children to show us the way to a happier Christmas observance. The ninth grade students in Scotch Plains High School, New Jersey, decided among themselves to pool all the money they had meant to spend on Christmas gifts for each other, in class and school observances, and give it to those who needed it more. With the advice and help of their local postmistress they chose the Muscular Dystrophy Fund as the object of their generosity.

In one Western public school the sixth graders were told that in many other lands the religious expression of Christmas was its most important element, and gift-giving a minor and more often separate part of the celebration, generally held on St. Nicholas Day. Since these lively youngsters had always been under the impression that gifts were the ultimate expression of Christmas, they were understandably surprised, and asked:

"How then should we celebrate the holiday?"

Their teacher asked them all to find the answer in the Bible: One boy wrote out this answer:

"I was hungered, and ye gave me meat: I was thirsty, and ye gave me drink . . . As ye have done it unto the least of these my brethren ye have done it unto me . . ."

That was a good beginning, the teacher told them, and suggested that they find the least of their brethren in their own town. They did, and began to collect their Christmas fund in a big, empty jar.

On Christmas Day there was enough in the jar for Christmas dinners and gifts for two families. And the children themselves took their gifts to both families. On the way back one of the teachers saw a little girl tightly clutching the empty mayonnaise jar that had held the Christmas fund.

"I'm going to put it under my tree at home," the little girl explained all aglow, "to remind me of the loveliest Christmas I've ever had."

Let such a Christ-like Christmas happen to you. You'll like it better than any Christmas you ever had.

Is all the fuss and bother worth it?
This family found out.

The Year We Had a "Sensible" Christmas
by Henry Appers

For as long as I could remember our family had talked about a sensible Christmas. Every year, my mother would limp home from shopping or she would sit beside the kitchen table after hours of baking, close her eyes, catch her breath and say, "This is the last time I'm going to exhaust myself with all this holiday fuss. Next year we're going to have a *sensible* Christmas."

And always my father, if he was within earshot, would agree. "It's not worth the time and expense."

While we were kids, my sister and I lived in dread that Mom and Dad would go through with their rash vows of a reduced Christmas. But if they ever *did,* we reasoned, there were several things about Christmas that we, ourselves, would like to amend. And two of these were, namely, my mother's Uncle Lloyd and his wife, Aunt Amelia.

Many a time Lizzie and I wondered why families had to have relatives, and especially why it was our fate to inherit Uncle Lloyd and Aunt Amelia. They were a sour and a formal pair who came to us every Christmas, bringing Lizzie and me handkerchiefs as gifts and expecting in return silence, respect, service and for me to surrender my bedroom

Lizzie and I had understood early that Great-uncle Lloyd was, indeed, a poor man, and we were sympathetic to this. But we dared to think that even poverty provided no permit for them to be stiff and unwarm and a nuisance in the bargain. Still we accepted Great-uncle Lloyd and Great-aunt Amelia as our lot and they were, for years, as much the tradition of Christmas as mistletoe.

Then came my first year in college. It must have been some perverse reaction to my being away, but Mom started it. *This* was to be the year of the sensible Christmas. "By not exhausting

12

ourselves with all the folderol,'' she wrote me, ''we'll at least have the energy and the time to appreciate Christmas.''

Dad, as usual, went along with Mom, but added his own touch. We were not to spend more than a dollar for each of our gifts to one another. ''For once,'' Dad said, ''we'll worry about the thought behind the gift, and not about its price.''

It was I who suggested that our sensible Christmas be limited to the immediate family, just the four of us. The motion was carried. Mom wrote a gracious letter to Great-uncle Lloyd explaining that what with my being away in school and for one reason and another we weren't going to do much about Christmas, so maybe they would enjoy it more if they didn't make their usual great effort to come. Dad enclosed a check, an unexpected boon.

I arrived home from college that Christmas wondering what to expect. A wreath on the front door provided a fitting nod to the season. There was a Christmas tree in the living room and I must admit that, at first, it made my heart twinge. Artificial, the tree was small and seemed without character when compared to the luxurious, forest-smelling firs of former years. But the more I looked at it, with our brightly wrapped dollar gifts under it, the friendlier it became and I began to think of the mess of real trees, and their fire threat, and how ridiculous, how really unnatural it was to bring a living tree inside a house anyway. Already the idea of a sensible Christmas was getting to me.

Christmas Eve Mom cooked a good but simple dinner and afterward we all sat together in the living room. ''This is nice,'' Lizzie purred, a-snuggle in the big cabbage rose chair.

''Yes,'' Dad agreed. ''It's quiet. I'm not tired out. For once, I think I can stay awake until church.''

''If this were last Christmas,'' I reminded Mom, ''you'd still be in the kitchen with your hours of 'last-minute' jobs. More cookies. More fruit cake.'' I recalled the compulsive way I used to nibble at Mom's fruit cake. ''But I never really liked it,'' I confessed with a laugh.

''I didn't know that,'' Mom said. She was thoughtful for a moment. Then her face brightened. ''But Aunt Amelia—how *she* adored it!''

''Maybe she was just being nice,'' Lizzie said undiplomatically.

Then we fell silent. Gradually we took to reading. Dad did slip off into a short snooze before church.

Christmas morning we slept late, and once up we breakfasted before advancing to our gifts. And what a time we had with those! We laughed merrily at our own originality and cleverness. I gave Mom a cluster-pin that I had fashioned out of aluminum measuring spoons and had adorned with rhinestones. Mother wore the pin all day, or at least, until we went out to Dempsey's.

At Dempsey, the best restaurant in town, we had a wonderful, unrushed feast. There was only one awkward moment just after the consomme was served. We started to lift our spoons. Then Dad suggested that we say grace and we all started to hold hands around the table as we always do at home, and then we hesitated and drew our hands back, and then in unison we refused to be intimidated by a public eating place and held hands and said grace.

Nothing much happened the rest of the day. In the evening I wandered into the kitchen, opened the refrigerator, poked around for a minute, closed the door and came back to the living room.

"That's a joke," I reported, with no idea at all of the effect my next remark would have. "I went out to pick at the turkey."

In tones that had no color, Mother spoke. "I knew that's what you went out there for. I've been waiting for it to happen."

No longer could she stay the sobs that now burst forth from her. "Kate!" Dad cried, rushing to her.

"Forgive me. Forgive me," Mom kept muttering.

"For what, dear? Please tell us."

"For this terrible, dreadful, sensible Christmas."

Each of us knew what she meant. Our Christmas had been as artificial as that Christmas tree; at some point the spirit of the day had just quietly crept away from us. In our efforts at common sense we had lost the reason for Christmas and had forgotten about others; this denied Him whose birthday it was all about. Each of us, we knew full well, had contributed to this selfishness, but Mom was taking the blame.

As her sobs became sniffles and our assurances began to take effect, Mom addressed us more coherently, in Mom's own special incoherent way. "I should have been in the kitchen last night instead of wasting my time," she began, covering up her sentimentality with anger. "So you don't like my fruit cake, Harry? Too bad. Aunt Amelia *really* adores it! And Elizabeth, even if she doesn't, you shouldn't be disrespectful to the old soul. Do you know who else loves my fruit cake? Mrs. Donegan down the street loves it. And she didn't get her gift from me this year. Why? Because we're being *sensible.*'' Then Mom turned on Dad, wagging her finger at him. "We can't afford to save on Christmas, Lewis! It shuts off the heart."

That seemed to sum it up.

Yet, Lizzie had another way of saying it. She put it in a letter to me at school, a letter as lovely as Lizzie herself. "Mom feels," Lizzie wrote, "that the strains and stresses are the birth pangs of Christmas. So do I. I'm certain that it is out of our efforts and tiredness and turmoil that some sudden, quiet, shining, priceless thing occurs each year and if all we produce is only a feeling as long as a flicker, it is worth the bother."

Just as my family came to call that The Christmas That Never Was, the next one became the Prodigal Christmas. It was the most festive, and the most frazzling time in our family's history—not because we spent any more money, but because we threw all of ourselves into the joy of Christmas. In the woods at the edge of town we cut the largest tree we'd ever had. Lizzie and I swathed the house in greens. Delicious smells came from the kitchen as Mom baked and baked and baked. . . . We laughed and sang carols and joked. Even that dour pair, Great-uncle Lloyd and Great-aunt Amelia were almost, but not quite gay. Still, it was through them that I felt that quick surge of warmth, that glorious "feeling as long as a flicker," that made Christmas meaningful.

We had just sat down in our own dining room and had reached out our hands to one another for our circle of grace. When I took Great-aunt Amelia's hand in mine, it happened. I learned something about her and giving that, without this Christmas, I might never have known.

The hand that I held was cold. I became aware of how gnarled her fingers were, how years of agonizing arthritis had twisted them. Only then did I think of the handkerchiefs that Lizzie and I had received this year, as in all the years before. For the first time I saw clearly the delicate embroidery, the painstaking needlework—Great-aunt Amelia's yearly gift of love to, and for, us.

An all-time favorite Spiritual Workshop feature from Guideposts on the eight steps of giving.

Is Your Heart in Your Giving?

HOW TO GIVE

The Bible abounds with advice on *how* to give. Paul tells us that we should give *not grudgingly, or of necessity: for God loveth a cheerful giver*. And in Matthew we are warned *to take heed that ye do not your alms before men, to be seen of them....*

These practical suggestions, and more, are echoed and restated by a remarkable man of the Middle Ages who put forth what he called "The Golden Ladder of Charity." Moses ben Maimon, who is known to us as Maimonides (1135–1204), was a Jewish philosopher-physician-astronomer-rabbi who greatly influenced the thinking and doctrine of not only his own religion but of Christian and Islamic thinking as well. In each of the steps of his Golden Ladder there is something for us to recognize—and to ponder.

Read through carefully the following eight steps, then, in the space designated, write in one or more personal gifts you have made in the past year that correspond to Maimonides' definition.

"*The first* and lowest degree is to give—but with reluctance or regret. This is the gift of the *hand* but not of the *heart*............
....

"*The second* is to give cheerfully, but not proportionately to the distress of the suffering ....
....

"*The third* is to give cheerfully, and proportionately, but not until we are solicited. ....
....

"*The fourth* is to give cheerfully, proportionately, and even unsolicited; but to put it in the poor man's hand, thereby exciting in him the painful emotion of shame...................................
....

"*The fifth* is to give charity in such a way that the distressed may receive the bounty and know their benefactor, without their being known to him. Such was the conduct of our ancestors, who used to tie up money in the hind-corners of their cloaks, so that the poor might take it unperceived ....
....

"*The sixth*, which rises still higher, is to know the objects of our bounty, but remain unknown to them. Such was the conduct of those of our ancestors who used to convey their charitable gifts into people's dwellings, taking care that their own persons should remain unknown ....

"*The seventh* is still more meritorious, namely, to bestow charity in such a way that the benefactor may not know the relieved persons, nor they the name of their benefactor. ....
....

"*The eighth* and most meritorious of all is to anticipate charity by preventing poverty; namely, to assist the reduced brother either by a considerable gift, or a loan of money, or by teaching him a trade, or by putting him in the way of business, so that he may earn an honest livelihood and not be forced to the dreadful alternative of holding up his hand for charity. This is the highest step and the summit of charity's Golden Ladder." ....
....

How many of the eight kinds of giving were you able to recount in your own experience? Did you find your list thinning out near the end? Most of us at Guideposts did.

AN EXPERIMENT

If you found your giving superficial, lacking the depth of true gifts from the heart, perhaps you would like to try an experiment this Christmas season. Here is the way it works:

In addition to your regular Christmas giving plan, or in place of it, make out a special list solely of gifts of self. It could include things you make, cook or grow; also visits to the lonely, gifts of time for babysitting, letters of appreciation. One of the best gifts of all could be the simple asking of forgiveness of someone you have wronged.

In preparing a Christmas card list, include people who would least expect but most appreciate a remembrance from you. Go

back through the years—what people have you lost track of?
Include them too. Then send one to the person you most dislike.
Use your imagination in creating a list that you think would most
please God.

KEEP TRYING

After Christmas go back to the Golden Ladder of Charity and
see if you can fill in the rungs near the top, especially six, seven
and eight. Make note of your successes and failures and vow to
improve your approach to giving in the months that lay ahead.
Ask God to help you be more sensitive to the needs of others and
less concerned about the cost to self.

In conclusion, remember that gracious giving requires no
special talent, nor large sums of money. It is compounded of the
heart and head acting together toward the perfect expression of
the spirit. It is love sharpened with imagination. The best gift is
always a portion of oneself.

A fretful housewife—hassled by unfinished Christmas chores—learns a lesson about getting things done.

One Step at a Time
by Carol Amen

I sat at the sewing machine staring at that pile of work.

The cut-out pieces of three bathrobes, a jumper and a blouse waited for me to transform them into gifts. I would never get them done by Christmas with everything else I had to do. Christmas was only eight days off now—only four of them school days in which to work secretly on these surprise projects.

I stared out the window which supplied a scant, gray winter's light to my sewing area, then back at the pile of work, trying to decide which garment to start on.

Actually, I felt like chucking the whole thing. I had wanted to sew in order to give my family exactly what they needed without spending too much money.

It seemed ironic to be making things for those I loved and hating every minute of it. What was the matter with me? I had been sitting there 15 minutes without sewing a single stitch.

I looked away from the sewing machine and peered out into the cold deserted street. Not even the usual hardy preschoolers were anywhere to be seen. And then, to my left, like a slow human snail, appeared Mr. Andrews bundled under coat, muffler and hat, and preceded by his cane.

Mr. Andrews was as new to the neighborhood as the rest of us—residents of about three months. He had told my son (size 14 bathrobe) that a stroke two years ago had left him helpless in bed for a long time. In recent months he had relearned to walk. "Just like a baby does," he had told my son. He had to practice every day or he'd regress. We met him often and always waved, but he could only nod slightly. It took every bit of concentration he could muster to command his legs and arms to coordinate his slow trek to the end of the street and back.

Now, curiously drawn by his jerky *tap-tap*, I watched him,

19

letting the robe pieces fall neglected into my lap. His progress was slow. Each step carried him about six inches forward.

How far it must seem to him to his goal—the end of the street, turn and shuffle slowly home, I thought. Then I gasped as I saw an obstacle. Because it was garbage collection day, neighbors had set their cans out by the street. But at the house directly across from us, they blocked the whole sidewalk. In order to get by, Mr. Andrews would have to step off the curb or balance himself on the slight incline of the driveway.

I watched him pause and study his problem. Half rising from my chair, I decided to run downstairs and outside to help, but he had started his detour alone. I stayed at the window hypnotized. Slowing from the already short, careful steps, Mr. Andrews began a series of even smaller inchings down the slope of the driveway. Once he tottered and almost fell, but instead of wasting breath calling out, he precariously steadied himself and proceeded. One foot and then the other—not always strong and sure but always determined, he moved on past the cans. Ever so slowly he edged back up the slope and onto the flat and ever so patiently on and on down the sidewalk.

I examined the pile of unattached bathrobe parts through a hot flush of shame. If I had not been stymied into inactivity by the overwhelmingness of my task, I could have had the first set of pockets on already. It embarrassed me to draw the comparison out fully. Here I sat with all my faculties intact except one—the will to begin, to take the first step. And there was Mr. Andrews.

He seemed to be speaking to me across the distance which separated us. *You can't get anywhere if you don't start,* floated one message on the gray winter day, and another was, *You can only go anywhere one step at a time.* I realized that my sewing machine, the same as Mr. Andrews' faltering legs, contained no magic. Work was required.

By the time his cane *tap-tapped* back in the other direction, I had the fronts and back attached with neat seams. I worked steadily the rest of that day and had size 14 finished and hidden away just as the school bus arrived.

I enjoyed the days that remained before Christmas. With a stack of carols on the record player, I hummed while stitching, and completed one gift each day. At exactly three o'clock of the Friday school was out, I wrapped the last outfit, my daughter's jumper and blouse, and placed it under the tree. If I had wasted five more minutes anywhere along the line, I'd never have finished in time.

FACING CHRISTMAS

I shall attend to my little errands of love
Early, this year,
So that the brief days before Christmas may be
Unhampered and clear
Of the fever of hurry. The breathless rushing
    that I have known in the past
Shall not possess me. I shall be calm in my soul
And ready at last
For Christmas: "The Mass of the Christ."
    I shall kneel and call out His name;
I shall take time to watch the beautiful light
Of a candle's flame;
I shall have leisure—I shall go out alone
From my roof and my door;
I shall not miss the silver silence of stars
As I have before;
And, oh, perhaps—If I stand there very still,
And very long—
I shall hear what the clamor of living has
    kept from me;
The Angels' song!

Grace Noll Crowell

Many people start the New Year
with this symbolic ritual.

Burning of the Greens

Not long ago, a Guideposts' friend, Lillian Elders of St. Louis, Missouri, sent us this account of an old family custom:

"It was soon after a New Year's Day years ago when I was a little girl. Mother called my sister, Rosie, and me to come into the yard. Snow had fallen the night before. Outside our house in the back yard lay the Christmas tree, stripped of decorations and with a few icicles clinging to the branches.

"Mother had dragged the tree to a small clearing, which was a safe distance from the house and where we occasionally burned leaves or trash.

" 'Stand back now!' she said. Then she struck a match, lit one of the branches. Soon the dry needles were crackling as the flames leaped from branch to branch.

"As the tree was being consumed, Mother said, 'Smell that fragrance. That's what you're to remember. The ashes you can forget. They will blow away.'

"When the tree was completely burned, the dark residue was in sharp contrast to the white snow. Mother pointed this out to us. 'Notice how much more white there is,' she said. 'There's always more white than black in life, but too many people see only the black things—that's what they remember most—the bad things that happen. You have to keep your eyes on the good things and remember them.'

"As the years passed, the symbolism of this New Year's ritual firmly fixed itself in my mind. Often it has been hard to keep my mind on the good in life. There were problems in my marriage, and I bore a child who had cerebral palsy.

"Yet, each New Year's after I have burned our Christmas tree, I sit down at my desk, take a clean sheet of paper and write, *Pleasant memories of 19—.* There has always been more fragrance than ashes."

A TRADITION FROM THE PAST

The editors of Guideposts believe that Mrs. Elders' ritual would make a good year-end habit. Of course, the "burning of the greens" is not a new idea, but one which comes from traditions of the past. It is usually done on January 6 (called Twelfth Night or Epiphany). Christians are believed to have first begun celebrating this day between 200 and 300 A.D. The word Epiphany comes from the Greek (meaning *appearance*) and signifies the coming of the Wise Men to the stable, the first disclosure of Christ to the Gentiles.

Fourteenth century Greeks celebrated it also as Theophany (appearance of God), and the Day of Lights and Illumination of Jesus.

In *All About American Holidays*, Maymie R. Krythe writes: "After the calendar change in Great Britain (1752), Twelfth Night celebrations lost in popularity in higher social circles. But the merriment continued in the rural districts, and included masques, wassailing the wheat fields, sprinkling apple trees with cider, and lighting bonfires....

"Aside from denominational observances, in recent years the United States has carried out a special Twelfth Night ceremony of its own that has become increasingly popular. On January 5, Christmas trees, wreaths, holly, and pine branches are taken to city parks; there they are set on fire with appropriate ritual, the flames of the great bonfires lighting up the winter sky....

"All join around the fire in singing the final Christmas carols; so this community event concludes the holiday season and celebrates Twelfth Night in happy modern fashion."

THE CUSTOM AS AN EXPERIMENT

The fact that many families, churches, organizations and communities still "burn greens" at the end of the Christmas season indicates that the tradition retains its meaningfulness. If you're interested in celebrating Twelfth Night this year, here are some suggestions:

First comes the written part. Like Mrs. Elders does, take paper and pen and find a peaceful place to sit and meditate. Let your mind go back over the past year, but do not dwell on the defeats and disappointments. Instead, write down the five most pleasant memories of the year.

Then prayerfully write down your goals and hopes for the new year. To make it specific, put down the month by which you hope certain aspirations come to pass.

Finally, there is the symbolism of the burning. If you can burn your Christmas tree outside without violating any local fire ordinances—fine. Otherwise, burn a small branch of green in a fireplace or in some other safe place. As the needles slowly turn to ash, consider this the unwanted residue of the past year. It will blow away. Let the fragrant smell of the green linger with you.

Finally, dedicate the new year to God and ask His blessing on your hopes and dreams.

The whole family got into the act—
and the whole family reaped the joy.

A Way to Make Christmas More Meaningful
by Catherine Marshall

At Thanksgiving time several years ago the question came up in one of our family sessions: How could the coming Christmas be made more meaningful? And it was the children who, as usual, went right to the heart of the matter: We had to find some way to think more about others.

"I think we should find a poor family and help them," said Jeff, our youngest. It was a good idea—but which poor family? Then one of us happened to mention the Stowes (not their real name), and instantly we were all excited. Actually the Stowes were not poverty-stricken; Mr. Stowe was a schoolteacher, but as such he symbolized to us all those respected citizens who serve selflessly and often with small pay. The Stowes had five children; they lived in a house much too small for such a large family; they were always to be counted on for community projects; and yet they never had those "extras" that many people take for granted.

"Could we give a present to each one?" Chester asked.

"At least," said Linda. "Maybe several."

"Clothes?" suggested Jeff, though actually he had toys and food more clearly in mind.

It was my husband, Len, who suggested that the Stowes not be told where the proposed gift came from. Len was thinking of the theme of Lloyd Douglas' *The Magnificent Obsession,* of the power that flows from giving anonymously.

That very day we gave ourselves research assignments. There was detective work to be done on clothing sizes, on the particular wishes and fancies of the five Stowe children. We set up a large cardboard box in the living room, and gradually, as Christmas neared, the box began to fill with presents. For Mrs. Stowe I bought a silk slip, lingerie I suspected she would never treat herself to; and without telling me, Len had a similar idea for Mr. Stowe—a handsome sport shirt. Gently, ever so reverently, the boys placed their own special gifts in the box—baseballs autographed by their particular major-league idols. So it went—clothes and games, toys and eats, personal treasures right up to the top.

Last of all came one of the few anonymous letters I have ever written. In it I explained to the Stowes that the point of the gifts was to try to say to them what their own unselfish giving meant to one family, as well as to others in the community.

Then on Christmas Eve came the most exciting time of all. Our whole family climbed into the station wagon and drove to the Stowes', where furtively, breathlessly, with a Halloween kind of fun, we left the box on the Stowe doorstep and cut out—but fast—for home!

I have marveled at how the excitement of giving can transform the atmosphere in our home to thoughtfulness, consideration, love, self-sacrifice. Since that first year we tried a project together, I have heard of many other families who find similar rewards in coordinated family giving. Some friends in New York invite an orphan home for the holidays every year; a family in Wisconsin makes toys for a children's hospital one year and "adopts" the lonely people in a retirement home the next.

When Miami, Florida, began to swell with Cubans fleeing from Castro, a family there devoted its Christmas to caring for a refugee family. Each year they choose their Christmas project keeping in mind the urgent community needs.

Every year as Christmas seems to come faster than ever, every year when that glorious event catches us all but unprepared for its surge of warmth and generosity, I am convinced that a family project can add a new dimension to family solidarity and new emphasis to what the Babe of Bethlehem means to the world.

Making Ready for Christmas

Where are all kinds of things we can do to remind ourselves of the spiritual side of Christmas, not just in church, but at home as well. The custom of the Advent wreath, found most often today in Lutheran and Catholic homes, is particularly appealing. This is a wreath with four candles standing in a circle of seasonal greens. Sometimes the wreath is fitted with ribbons so it can be hung, but many like it best as a centerpiece for the dining room table.

A Baptist family in Hightstown, New Jersey, has a permanent Advent wreath. Guideposts received a letter recently from Mary Ann Bohrs. "Each Sunday of Advent," she wrote, "we light a new candle until, by Christmas, all four candles are blazing. Then each evening we light the candles again and read the ancient prophecies."

What a wonderful sight! Can't you picture that family, Harry and Mary Ann and their two little boys gathered around the table, the candlelight flickering dramatically, every one of them listening intently to those tremendous Old Testament words? Those are words that make you sense the long centuries of waiting, that make you experience a mounting excitement about His coming... *The voice of him that crieth in the wilderness, prepare ye the way of the Lord*. And the tension grows in that family until there comes at last that quiet moment in the Gospels when... *a child is born in Bethlehem*....

Mrs. Bohrs closed her letter in a lovely way. "As I put our Christmas decorations back in the attic each year," she said, "I pray that the Lord Jesus be in our lives, not just in our festivals, not just over the mantel, but in our hearts."

Certainly it is our hearts that provide the key to Christmas each year. Virginia Rootes Juergens of Dallas, Texas, wrote a story about a lady named Mrs. Mason and her creative approach to the holiday. Mrs. Mason, it seems, lived in the small Texas

27

town where Virginia grew up. Mrs. Mason was an elderly woman with very little money, but her Christmas preparations were extravagant.

Weeks before Christmas every year, she plotted and planned for what she called her "Lordly gifts." Wandering around the little town, the old lady would select three people to give a gift to, three people from whom she expected nothing in return. A lot of thought would go into each present, a lot of work, a lot of self-denial—and a lot of pleasure.

"I just can't think of my third Lordly gift," Mrs. Mason said to Virginia one time when she visited the Mason cottage during this period of preparation. "You know, child, we have to give something worthy. Don't forget, it's the birthday of God's Son."

That year Mrs. Mason had decided already on a pair of shoes for her first gift and had saved the necessary money. Her second gift was to be a week's mending of a poor family's clothes. (Mrs. Mason did not disclose the names of the recipients-to-be.) But her third gift, as always, seemd to give Mrs. Mason trouble. "I just can't think of anything, child," she said to Virginia, "at least nothing Lordly."

Before Christmas, of course, just as Virginia knew she would, Mrs. Mason made her momentous decision and carried it through. "Only later did I discover what her gift was," Mrs. Juergens wrote. "She came in three afternoons a week to 'baby-sit' (a term unknown then) and helped my sister Helen and me make cookies while my hard-working teacher-mother was away."

Mrs. Mason knew what Christmas was all about. She approached it seriously and gaily, indeed it was a birthday to her, and her gifts were Lordly because they were gifts to the Christ Child. No one had to tell Mrs. Mason *As ye have done it unto one of the least of these my brethren, ye have done it unto me.*

So Christmas is coming again. This year during these meaningful weeks of Advent, let's all bring out the trappings of the holiday, but let's keep in mind what significance they can have just as the Bohrs family does with its Advent wreath. This year let's prepare for Christmas as Mrs. Mason did, as we would for "the birthday of God's Son." Let's be creative. And let's make ready our homes, our hearts, our world, to receive Him.

A CHRISTMAS PRAYER

Loving Father, help us remember the birth of Jesus, that we may share in the song of the angels, the gladness of the shepherds, and the worship of the wise men.

Close the door of hate and open the door of love all over the world.

Let kindness come with every gift and good desires with every greeting.

Deliver us from evil by the blessing which Christ brings, and teach us to be merry with clear hearts.

May the Christmas morning make us happy to be Thy children, and the Christmas evening bring us to our beds with grateful thoughts, forgiving and forgiven, for Jesus' sake. Amen!

Robert Louis Stevenson

"God is not niggardly," she told John.
He agreed to pray for a handsome coat.

The Christmas Overcoat
by Ada Shaw

The overcoat was almost constantly in my mind as I scurried around Chicago on Christmas errands.

Winter had begun early that year in the middle of the Depression and by the Christmas season, it had set in with frightening stubbornness. My husband, John Shaw, an itinerant Evangelical minister of the Gospel, was one of those provoking saints who actually does live by the spirit. I was more practical by nature (and partly by necessity). Somehow we managed to pay our rent on the one-room apartment within walking distance of the Loop; somehow we managed to buy enough food for ourselves and the numerous "brothers" who happened in, often desperately hungry.

I did odd jobs to augment our income, and the women for whom I worked often gave me fairly good castoffs. But John had no overcoat. Daily I met him as he came in out of the bitter weather, blue with cold and shaking with chills. I'd make him a cup of hot tea and wrap him in blankets until his frail body could relax. He'd smile and say, "God's in His heaven! All's right with the world!"

He believed it, for his prayers were childlike in their faith. One day, when we were down to our last heel of bread, a pathetically young mission worker sat hopefully awaiting a meal. John walked into our alcove bedroom to pray. Almost immediately there came a knock at the door and a baker from the little shop near us handed in a great basket of rolls and cake.

I called it coincidence, or possibly providence; but John called it an answer to prayer.

Christmas came even closer. One day when the snow swept past our windows, I asked, as we finished a bowl of potato soup, "How about that overcoat you need, John?"

"I almost forgot." He stood up, saying, "I'll go right now and pray for it."

The bedroom alcove was chilly, and I knew John soon would be kneeling on the worn rug beside the iron bedstead.

"Listen, John," I said, taking him by both thin arms and looking straight into his bright eyes, "what kind of an overcoat are you going to pray for?"

He looked startled.

"Are you going to pray for some thin old garment that has already outworn its usefulness? Just last night at the Gospel Mission, you said, 'God is not niggardly!' "

Into John's bright eyes came that merry, quizzical smile that endeared him to everybody— as if he had his own private joke but would share it just with you.

"I shall pray for a very warm coat," he promised me. "Perhaps I shall even specify that it be handsome."

The weather moderated somewhat that afternoon and, too restless to stay in, I went for a walk. Snow was falling. The Christmas spirit was in the air everywhere. Carol music came from the store windows. Irresistibly, I was drawn all the way down to Marshall Field's department store, and furthermore, to their overcoat display.

I explained that I'd like to look at a fine coat of ministerial conservatism. The moment I saw the coat he clerk offered I knew it was John's. I smoothed the rich broadcloth, felt of the black satin lining and velvet collar. Yes, this was John's coat.

I gave his name and address, "Will you hold it?" I asked. "At least until Christmas?"

"Certainly, madam."

While I was in the store, it had seemed the most natural thing in the world to be choosing a coat for my husband, as any wife of a busy man might do. But out on the street again, with the wind whipping afresh from Lake Michigan, I would have shed tears except that I knew they'd freeze on my face.

John was waiting for me. He had lit the stove-top oven into which I had placed a couple of baking potatoes and a small meatloaf. The tea-kettle hummed extravagantly. In John's face were no lines of worry, and I felt a contentment I had no right to feel. I made a pan of biscuits and opened a jar of precious jam.

"What are we celebrating?" John inquired.

"Your overcoat," I answered.

"To be sure," he agreed.

I had just put the kitchen end of the room to rights when the buzzer sounded and up the stairs, puffing, came Mr. Carston. He was a very rich man, interested in the rehabilitation of the unfortunate and he had attended John's meeting the night before. He wanted to arrange a series of just such meetings, and he was slightly provoked that no one had answered his summons when he stopped by earlier in the afternoon. John admitted he had been home.

I followed Mr. Carston out on the landing.

"I can tell you why John didn't hear you this afternoon, Mr. Carston," I said. "He was in the bedroom praying—praying for an overcoat."

"Praying for an overcoat?" Mr. Carston's whole being demanded why a spiritual man should pray for a material thing. It was fitting and proper to pray for grace, for the strength to endure, even for bread—but an overcoat!

"I'll see what I can do," he said uneasily. "I may have something in my wardrobe—something that could be cut down."

He was a very large man, and John was slight. I hesitated and tried to keep my voice steady.

"John has prayed for a *new* overcoat, Mr. Carston," I revealed. "He has even prayed that it be warm and handsome. It isn't often that he asks for anything for himself, but he knows God is not niggardly."

"Well . . ." Mr. Carston began, then he stopped uncertainly. "Evidently you have some idea . . ."

I took the "will hold" slip from my blouse pocket and handed it to him.

"I'll not promise anything," he said, but he kept the slip.

That was Thursday night.

On the day before Christmas the overcoat was delivered to John. When he lifted it out of its handsome box, he glowed as though he were lit within.

I never told John. For a long time I even thought that it was I who had manipulated the wheels of chance, and I said to myself: "God helps him who helps himself."

But as I grew older I began to wonder. Could it be that God *had* answered John's prayer? Could it be that He simply used me and Mr. Carston as instruments? I think so . . . I hope so . . . I believe so.

Section II
Christmas—A Time for Healing

Christmas is a time for healing,
When disagreers and disagreements meet,
When long-time wounds are mended
And love moves hatred to retreat.

An answered newspaper ad
brings a double blessing.

The Christmas I Loaned My Son
by Mrs. N. H. Muller

Q.: Is there any place where we can borrow a little boy three or four years old for the Christmas holidays? We have a nice home and would take wonderful care of him and bring him back safe and sound. We used to have a little boy, but he couldn't stay, and we miss him so when Christmas comes.—N.M.
A.: If anyone has a little boy to lend over Christmas, write to this column as early as possible, marking "Christmas" on outside of envelope.

As I read the above appeal in our local newspaper something happened to me: for the first time since my husband's death I thought of grief as belonging to someone else. I read and reread the letter to the editor. Should I answer it? Could I answer it?

When I received word from Washington that my husband had been killed in service overseas, I'd taken my little son and moved back to the tiny village of my birth.

I'd gone to work to help support my son and time had helped to erase a few scars in my heart and to soften the blow of my husband's passing. But there were special times when the ache would return and loneliness would engulf me. Birthdays, our wedding anniversary and holidays. . . .

This particular Christmas the old pain was returning when my eyes caught the appeal in the newspaper column.

We used to have a little boy, but he couldn't stay and we miss him so when Christmas comes. . . .

I, too, knew what missing was, but I had my little boy. I knew how empty the sparkle of Christmas is unless you see it by the candles of joy in a child's eyes.

I answered the appeal. The writer of the letter was a widower who lived with his mother. He had lost his beloved wife and his little son the same year.

That Christmas my son and I shared a joyous day with the widower and his mother. Together, we found a happiness that we doubted would ever be ours again.

But the best part is that this joy was mine to keep throughout the years and for each of the 10 Christmases since. You see, the man who wrote the letter became my husband.

THE JOY OF GIVING

Somehow not only for Christmas
But all the long year through,
The joy that you give to others
Is the joy that comes back to you.
And the more you spend in blessing
The poor and lonely and sad,
The more of your heart's possessing
Returns to make you glad.

John Greenleaf Whittier

"And then one of them came up to me—I'll never
forget it—this little boy came up and he stood
there and he stroked the sleeve of my coat."

When Christmas Came Again
by Dina Donohue

Many people knew that Frank Hinnant had no use for Christmas,
but few understood the reasons why he had shut Christmas out of
his heart.

As the head of his own multimillion dollar contracting business, Frank discouraged Yuletide office parties each year. He
gave no Christmas bonuses. It was enough that his employees
received pay increases when merited and fringe benefits more
generous than any firm in town.

His wife, Adele, was of a different fabric. She loved Christmas and she longed to celebrate it fully, with all the fuss she
could stir up. It was the one chronic disagreement the Hinnants
had. Each December they renewed the argument. Adele wanted
decorations, a tree, gifts, even parties for employees—and Frank
said, emphatically, "No." Dutifully he would go along to other
people's parties, he would go to Christmas services as usual, and
for Adele there would always be a string of pearls or a costly, but
tasteful, pin—but beyond that, "Nonsense," Frank would say,
"Christmas is for children!"

And that is precisely the reason Frank Hinnant had locked
Christmas out of his heart—children.

One morning, a brisk, December day, Frank decided to walk
to work. He did this occasionally, varying his route each time.
Frank was a man with a giant curiosity, fascinated by people,
where they lived, and how. This morning, reaching mid-town, he
noticed a cluster of people standing in front of Leeson's Department Store. They were looking at the Christmas displays, each
on a different theme.

One window had a manger scene. Frank looked at the creche:
at Mary, Joseph and the shepherd in colorful costumes; the

donkey, cow and sheep—all were life-size. And there was the Child.

Frank turned away.

He started to move on. As he did, a sign across the street caught his fleeting attention.

"Holy Innocents Home"—huge golden letters framed the arched doorway of an old brownstone building surrounded by a forbidding iron fence. Frank had only half noticed this building before. Even now it had a way of shrinking into the urban landscape.

"Holy Innocents... Holy Innocents...." Frank repeated the name in his mind. He stood there staring at the orphanage across the street, and yet he was seeing something else, something far beyond, a long ago morning in Sunday school. There was Miss Raymond, a skinny woman with black hair pulled back into a knot, and Miss Raymond was telling the class about King Herod and all the male children under two, "... and the wicked king had had these little children slaughtered because he feared the Baby Jesus...."

"The Holy Innocents," Frank said to himself. "That's odd, you don't hear about them much. Christmas is just this sentimental mush, like Adele's joy-on-earth stuff. There's more to Christmas than syrup. There's misery too."

Frank turned back to the windows of Leeson's. He looked at the smiles on the benign faces of Mary and Joseph. But what about the parents of the infants who had died? What about *their* faces?

And for the millionth time Frank remembered the desolation of the day that David had died.

David had been 18 months old. In the 22 years since then, Frank had not been able to bring himself to mention his son's name.

Frank walked on towards his office. At the corner he turned and looked back. "The Holy Innocents," he said, almost out loud.

Impulsively he struck out on a new course. An idea had come to him. Quickly he covered the four blocks to the public library, then up the steps and in, arriving at the information desk to fairly demand one reference book after another. Librarians began to heap tomes in front of him and Miss Summerwell herself stayed by his side to render assistance.

"Holy Innocents," reported Miss Summerwell, book in hand, finger pointing. "Their feast day is celebrated on December 28 by the Anglican and Roman Catholic churches, on December 29 by the Greek Orthodox church. They are among the early martyrs. . . ."

The information mounted, some of it conflicting. Some sources stated that thousands of infants had been slaughtered by Herod, others reported only a few. Frank was most impressed by the historian who very carefully deduced that since only about 2,000 people were living then in Bethlehem, no more than 20 children had been killed.

"Imagine that," he shouted to Miss Summerwell, "only 20 children!"

Very politely Miss Summerwell asked this extraordinary man to try to keep his voice a little lower.

When Frank left the public library that day he still did not go to his office. He headed back to Holy Innocents Home.

That evening, Frank and Adele dined alone. It was a leisurely dinner, yet Frank was ill at ease. He was searching for the right moment, the right phrases to use when he told Adele what, sooner or later, he had to tell her.

"I had an odd kind of day," he plunged in finally. "I went to visit an orphanage."

Adele wouldn't have been more taken aback if Frank had said he'd flown to the Hebrides for lunch, but, having lived with Frank a long time, she registered only the mildest curiosity.

"It's that bastille of an orphanage across from Leeson's," Frank ambled on. "Really a dungeon, dear, cramped and dismal. . . ."

Adele was fascinated. Frank was building up to something. Now he told about the walk downtown, about the creche at Leeson's. At last he told her about his visit to the orphanage itself. "It made me realize how little I really know about kids. What strange little ugly creatures they are! When I went in they stood around looking at me like I was a movie star, not one of them saying anything. Later one of them came up to me—I'll never forget it—this little boy came up and he stood there and he stroked the sleeve of my coat."

Adele was quiet. It was her eyes that urged him to continue. But Frank was embarrassed now. "You know full well what I've always said about Christmas," he blustered. "Christmas is for children!"

"Yes, you've always said that."

"Well, it's about time people started doing something for them. Today I gave that place some money. They're going to build a wing with it."

Adele was swept away by the kindness of this man she had loved so long. She thought she knew him completely, but she was unprepared for his next announcement, "They're going to name the wing for David."

It was the first time in 22 years that Adele had heard Frank mention their only son's name. It made her do something she never did when Frank was around. She wept.

Frank never told her about that moment. He never told her how, as he held her in his arms, he saw again something he had envisioned for the first time that afternoon. He saw a room full of children. There were 20 of them playing in a bright new wing at Holy Innocents. But now, suddenly, instead of 20, there were 21.

THE BALLAD OF BEFANA

Befana the Housewife, scrubbing her pane,
Saw three old sages ride down the lane,
Saw three gray travelers pass her door—
Gaspar, Balthazar, Melchior.
"Where journey you, sirs?" she asked of them.
Balthazar answered, "To Bethlehem,
For we have news of a marvelous thing.
Born in a stable is Christ the King."
"Give Him my welcome!"
Then Gaspar smiled,
"Come with us, mistress, to greet the Child."
"Oh, happily, happily would I fare,
Were my dusting through and I'd polished the stair."
Old Melchior leaned on his saddle horn.
"Then send but a gift to the small Newborn."
"Oh, gladly, gladly I'd send Him one,
Were the hearthstone swept and my weaving done.
"As soon as ever I've baked my bread,
I'll fetch Him a pillow for His head,
And a coverlet too," Befana said.
"When the rooms are aired and the linen dry,

I'll look at the Babe.''
But the Three rode by.
She worked for a day and a night and a day,
Then, gifts in her hands, took up her way.
But she never could find where the Christ Child lay.
And still she wanders at Christmastide,
Houseless, whose house was all her pride,
Whose heart was tardy, whose gifts were late;
Wanders, and knocks at every gate,
Crying, "Good people, the bells begin!
Put off your toiling and let love in.''

Phyllis McGinley

Vicki quit talking when her baby sister arrived and it took a special sight at Christmas before she spoke again.

A Moment Beyond Words
by Eleanor Cicak

Vicki, my three-year-old daughter, was a noisy, prattling youngster until her sister, Claudia, was born. Then Vicki became suddenly silent. Although she understood all that was said, she spoke no word—not even "Mama" when she wanted me.

The silence was frightening, but doctors found nothing organically wrong. "An emotional block," one said.

Where do parents turn in such a crisis? We tried to get help for Vicki at many hospitals, clinics, and schools, but were turned down again and again. "She's too young." "There's a long waiting list." "She doesn't fit." The answers gave us little hope. Finally one doctor recommended Lenox Hill Hospital in New York City, and we entered Vicki in their clinic and nursery school.

We met other parents there and learned we were not alone in our trouble. Together we formed a group—to help further the good work the clinic was accomplishing with our children. And every day I took Vicki to the nursery school.

At home I taught her about God by reciting prayers to her and reading stories from the Bible and Jesus' life in gaily colored picture books. Vicki had one favorite picture—Mary holding the Baby Jesus. She would often open the book and point to the picture—smiling.

Vicki had some definite dislikes, too; and, for some reason, every time I opened the door of a church, she would draw back as if frightened of the darkness or the quiet. I did not press the point.

Two years passed. Vicki still had not spoken; but her behavior was improving and she appeared happier. One day, just before Christmas, as we passed our church, I impulsively turned and mounted the steps regardless of the tug on my hand.

Inside, the church was as silent as Vicki. Her little hand still clutching mine, we walked down the long aisle and paused before the rows of candles flickering inside red glasses. Suddenly Vicki tugged with such urgency at my hand that I looked down at her.

I saw wonder in her face as she pointed to the statue of the Virgin and Child. Then suddenly Vicki broke her silence of two years with these words:

"Look! Baby Jesus."

TIME OF ENCHANTMENT

On Christmas Eve, the story says, an enchantment falls upon the earth. It is a time when the Spirit of a new-born Child whose name is Love, possesses the world. The way to Christmas lies through an ancient gate, patterned after a sheepfold and guarded by angels with star dust in their hair. It is a little gate, child-high, child-wide, and there is a password: Peace on earth to men of good will. May you, this Christmas, become as a little child again and enter into His kingdom.

Angelo Patri

There is a contagion about Christmas
that can transform even . . .

A Lonely Cafeteria
by Florence Mauthe

On Christmas morning the cafeteria looked sterile—white table-
cloths, cold tiled floors, and white-uniformed counter girls and
busboys bustling about. Even the Christmas tree set up in the
corner did nothing to dispel my feelings of depression as I
arrived to begin my duties as supervisor.

The first customers arriving for breakfast were the elderly
residents of the hotel. This morning, as they did each day, they
put their food on their trays, paid the cashier and then each went
to a lonely separate table. One or two ventured a hesitant
"Merry Christmas," but there was no warmth in their voices.

Forgetting my own resentment at having to leave a warm home
to work on Christmas, I began to walk among the tables,
nodding to customers and trying to smile the "Merry Christmas"
I did not really feel. Then from the corner of my eye, I spotted
four of the busboys in a huddle. Thinking they were dawdling, I
started to reprimand them, but before I could speak out, I heard
some barely audible sounds:

Our Father, Which art in Heaven
Hallowed be Thy name.

The boys were singing, and now the melody rose and flowed
through the room, quiet but beautiful in muted harmony.

Faces came alive with surprise and reverence. One of the boys
turned off the lights. Only the tree glowed then, its lights
reflecting the gay bulbs and tinsel. The prayer ended, and the
room was hushed. Someone sighed. Then the boys sang *Silent
Night*, *Adeste Fideles* and *Hark, the Herald Angels Sing*. As they
sang, they moved about the room, working and encouraging the
timid to join in the caroling.

When breakfast was over, the conversation was warm and
animated and the diners moved reluctantly from the room.

Someone shouted, "Merry Christmas," and his words were echoed all down the line.

Over these tired, lonely, old faces had swept the transforming spirit of Christmas—a spirit that never pales, never ages, never loses its power.

Singing a solo in the Christmas cantata
was the last thing Herbie planned to do.

The C-C-Choir Boy
by Fred Bauer

Everyone was surprised—everyone except Mrs. Brown, the choir director—when Herbie showed up in November to rehearse for the church's annual Christmas cantata.

Mrs. Brown wasn't surprised because she had persuaded Herbie to "at least try." That was an accomplishment, for lately he had quit trying nearly everything—reciting in class, playing ball or even asking his brothers or sisters to pass the potatoes.

It was easy to understand: He stuttered. Not just a little, either, and sometimes when his tongue spun on a word, like a car on ice, the kids laughed. Not a big ha-ha laugh, but you can tell when people are laughing at you even if you're only nine.

Mrs. Brown had figured Herbie could sing with the other tenors—Charley and Billy—and not have any trouble, which is exactly the way it worked. Billy was given the only boy's solo and the rest of the time the three of them sang in unison, until Charley contracted the measles. Even so, Billy had a strong voice and Herbie knew he could follow him.

At 7:15, the night of the cantata, a scrubbed and combed Herbie arrived at church, wearing a white shirt, a new blue and yellow bow tie and his only suit, a brown one with high-water pant legs. Mrs. Brown was waiting for him at the door.

"Billy is home in bed with the flu," she said. "You'll have to sing the solo." Herbie's thin face grew pale.

"I c-c-can't," he answered.

"We need you," Mrs. Brown insisted.

It was unfair. He wouldn't do it. She couldn't make him. All of these thoughts tumbled through Herbie's mind until Mrs. Brown told him this:

"Herbie, I know you can do this—with God's help. Across from the choir loft is a stained-glass window showing the

48

manger scene. When you sing the solo, I want you to sing it only to the Baby Jesus. Forget that there is anyone else present. Don't even glance at the audience." She looked at her watch. It was time for the program to begin.

"Will you do it?"

Herbie studied his shoes.

"I'll t-t-try," he finally answered in a whisper.

A long 20 minutes later, it came time for Herbie's solo. Intently, he studied the stained-glass window. Mrs. Brown nodded, and he opened his mouth, but at that exact instant someone in the congregation coughed.

"H-H-Hallelujah," he stammered. Mrs. Brown stopped playing and started over. Again, Herbie fixed his eyes on the Christ Child. Again, he sang.

"Hallelujah, the Lord is born," his voice rang out, clear and confident. And the rest of his solo was just as perfect.

After the program, Herbie slipped into his coat and darted out a back door—so fast that Mrs. Brown had to run to catch him. From the top of the steps, she called, "Herbie, you were wonderful. Merry Christmas."

"Merry Christmas to you, Mrs. Brown," he shouted back. Then, turning, he raced off into the night through ankle-deep snow—without boots. But then he didn't really need them. His feet weren't touching the ground.

Nearly two thousand years ago their heavenly
voices heralded the birth of God's son.

The Night the Angels Sang
by Jim Bishop

Joseph apologized to Mary. He was sorry that the Hospice of
Chamaan had no room for her and ashamed that he had failed her
in this hour.

Mary studied her husband, a tender smile on her face. She told
her husband that he had not failed her; he had been good and
tender and lawful. Mary looked around at the haltered cattle, the
few lambs, some asses and a camel. If it is the will of God, she
said, that His son be born in a place like this, she would not
question it.

She asked Joseph to go outside and tend the fire and to remain
there until she called him. Joseph did so, heating the water and
praying . . . when he heard a tiny, thin wail. He wanted to rush in
at once. He got to his feet, and moved no further. She would
call.

"Joseph." It was a soft call, but he heard it. He hurried
inside.

Mary smiled at her husband as he bent far over to look. There
among the cloths, he saw the tiny red face of an infant. This,
said Joseph to himself, is the one of whom the angels spoke. He
dropped to his knees.

Down in the valley, sheep huddled against the chill—when the
deep night sky was split with light. The sleeping shepherds
awakened and, in fear, hid their eyes in the folds of their
garments. Then, an angel appeared in bodily form, standing in
air over the valley.

"Do not fear," the angel said slowly. "I bring you good news
of great joy. A Saviour, who is the Lord Messias, was born to
you today in David's town. And this shall serve you as a token:
You will find an infant wrapped in swaddling clothes and cradled
in a manger."

There was nothing frightening in that news. It had been promised by God a long time ago. The shepherds knew that they were not sleeping. This thing was happening; happening to lonely and despised men in a valley beneath Bethlehem.

They were still dwelling on the wonders of God and His works when the angel was joined by hundreds of others, who appeared brightly in the night sky, and began to sing in a heavenly chorus:

"Glory to God in the heaven above,
  and on earth peace to men of good will."

> Because of his blind daughter, Luigi would
> have nothing to do with the church.

The Stubborn Unbeliever
by Arthur Gordon

More than seven hundred years ago in the little village of Greccio in Italy there lived a man who was at war with God. His name was Luigi, and he had his reasons.

He was a strong man, black-eyed, hot-tempered, with wonderful sensitive hands. From childhood, he had had the gift of shaping wood into marvelous imitations of life. And for a long time, he accepted this talent with gratitude, as a sign of God's favor. But the day came when Luigi cursed heaven. It was the day that he learned his daughter—his only child—had been born blind.

After that day, Luigi went no more to the little church on the hill. He refused to allow prayers in his house. His child had been called Maria, after the Queen of Heaven. He changed her name to Rosa.

His wife pleaded in vain; nothing could move him. "I will have nothing to do," he said, "with a God who condemns innocent children to darkness!" To an artist, blindness is like a sentence of death.

Then in mid-December, in the year 1207, a muletrain came through Greccio. Among the treasures on display was a magnificent piece of ivory. As soon as he saw it, Luigi had the thought that he would carve it into a doll—a *bambino*—for his little girl. In three days it was finished. Life-sized, smiling; the ivory *bambino* seemed almost to breathe. Luigi told no one about the ivory image except his wife, and he told her only because he wanted her to make some clothes for the doll.

Meanwhile, in the village, everyone was talking about the young friar who had come from a neighboring town to preach. No one could say exactly what it was about his preaching, but people came away with an extraordinary sense of peace, as if all the anger and pain of living had been lifted from their hearts.

Luigi's wife heard the young friar preach, and she begged her husband to come to church with her. But Luigi shook his head. "When this God of yours shows me that He can cure blindness, then I will believe in Him."

He would not let his wife take Rosa, either. But she wanted desperately to bring her child into some sort of contact with the love and warmth that seemed to flow from the young friar. On Christmas Eve, she thought of a way.

When, by chance, Luigi went into his workshop, his shout of fury brought the servants running. The ivory *bambino* was gone. From a terrified maid, Luigi learned that his wife had taken the ivory image to the church to have it blessed.

Out into the street and up the hill stalked Luigi, black anger in his heart. But before he could reach the church door, a cavalcade swept up, three young nobles, richly dressed, then six mounted servants, and finally two carts loaded with animals: sheep, goats, oxen, a donkey.

A young man in a purple coat sprang down from his horse. "Francesco Bernardone!" he shouted. "We got your message and we are here!"

Luigi spoke roughly to one of the servants, "Who is this Francesco Bernardone that you seek here in Greccio?"

The servant pointed. "That is he—the friar!" The church door had opened, and a slender, brown-clad figure had come out. "Welcome my friends," he said smiling, "and God's peace be upon you all."

'We've brought the animals," the young noble said. "But really, Francesco, how long are you going to play this farce? Assisi isn't the same without you!"

Luigi tightened his hold on the servant's shoulder. "Who is this man?"

The servant shrugged despairingly. "In Assisi, until not long ago, he was my master's friend and drinking companion. Now, they say, he preaches the word of God. It is very strange."

Other servants were unloading the carts, where the frightened animals reared and plunged. "A moment please," the friar said. He walked over to the nearest cart and laid his hand on one of the oxen. "Be calm, there, Brother Ox. And you, Sister Sheep, do not baa so pitifully."

And even as he spoke, the animals grew calm and still.

A hush seemed to fall upon the people who had gathered. In this sudden quiet, the friar said to the young man in the purple cloak, "Come into the church, Lorenzo. I want to show you my manger scene."

The young man hesitated, "I am no believer, Francesco."

"All the more reason for coming," the little friar said. He turned back into the church, and all the animals followed him, and the people, too. Even Luigi followed, because he could not help it.

Inside near the altar was a shelter made of green boughs, and in the shelter was a manger. Luigi knew what it contained, for a woman was kneeling near it; her face beautiful in the candle-light. The woman was his wife.

Without being led, without being driven, the animals gathered around the manger. Then the little friar stood before them. "I was going to read you the Christmas story from the Gospel," he said. "But my nativity scene makes me so happy that I am going to sing it to you."

No one who heard his song ever forgot its sweetness. He told the ageless story of the angels and the shepherds, of the Wise Men. Even the animals seemed to be listening. And Luigi was prepared to believe that they could understand the words too, because an even greater miracle was taking place within himself. His anger seemed to be fading away. A strange peace had come upon him.

Nor was his the only heart that was being changed. The young man in the purple cloak moved forward. From around his neck he took a chain of gold, and he knelt down and put it beside the manger. And after him his companions came and put down gifts.

Luigi felt a touch on his arm. Looking around, he saw the little friar smiling at him. "You wondered if God could cure blindness," the friar said. "Well, we are watching Him do it, are we not?"

Luigi did not answer, for there was a tightness in his throat. He could see the villagers crowding forward to look into the manger, and the awe and wonder in their faces as they gazed upon his handiwork. Afterwards, there were those who swore that the ivory *bambino* stirred and smiled and lifted his arms to them. But this, no doubt, was the flickering candlelight.

Then the friar said, "Please thank your daughter for the loan of her Christmas present. And now you may take it back."

Luigi shook his head. "It is where it belongs. Let it stay."

The friar said, "Tomorrow is Christmas. Your little girl would be disappointed."

"No," said Luigi, "I will make her another *bambino*. I will carve her a whole manger scene, so that Ro . . . I mean Maria, will have Christmas at her finger tips whenever she wants it."

So Luigi went home, leaving behind the ivory *bambino* with St. Francis of Assisi in what, according to legend, was the first actual creche. Hand in hand with his wife, he walked back down the hill. And he worked all night with gratitude in his heart because he knew that in his house blindness had indeed been cured—not his daughter's, but his own.

The Boy with the Lonely Eyes
by Frank Graves*

The first time I met Jim Patterson, I had the feeling that he was going to spit at me. Contempt, that was the impression this 15-year-old boy gave. He looked with suspicion at the hand I offered; if the judge hadn't been there I doubt he would have bothered to shake it.

But there was something else about him: his eyes. They were so sad, so passive, so melancholy. Without question, he had the loneliest eyes I have ever seen.

So this was the boy the court wanted me to take back to Boys Republic! Obviously Jim Patterson didn't want to come. And to tell the truth, at first I didn't want him there. I'd had plenty of experience with his quiet, surly type. It's always easier, I said to myself, with the steam-spouters.

Certainly we didn't have to accept him. Our farm-school community is a private undertaking, held together by the generosity of friends and held up, often, by its own bootstraps. It's non-profit and non-sectarian and though most of its 125 14- to 18-year-olds are indeed wards of the California juvenile courts, we only accept those troubled boys who we think will benefit from our type of life. Self-government, self-discipline, work, sunshine—these are the things that Boys Republic, since 1907, has represented.

Later, alone with me, the judge said, "Take him out there with you, Mr. Graves. It's hard to get him to talk, I know, but he's bright and I have a strong, experienced hunch that he's eager to work. He's hungry to be himself."

The boy's record showed a bizarre upbringing. Both his mother and father were alcoholics; he was their only child.

---

*Director of Boys Republic, Chino, California

Sometimes they had beaten him, but what was worse, they neglected him. They'd lock him in his room without food for days on end. When he stole money from a cash register one day, his peculiar family background was revealed, and the court placed him in a foster home.

All had gone well for awhile. Jim seemed to warm to normal home life; apparently he liked his foster parents. And then he was caught in a department store stealing an electric hair dryer; he said that he had wanted to give it to his foster mother for her birthday. His fate now lay at the discretion of the court and the court wanted him to go to Boys Republic.

While driving the 40 miles from Los Angeles to Chino that January afternoon, I soon gave up trying to draw Jim Patterson into conversation. He sat there staring out of the window as though he were being kidnapped. He wasn't a handsome lad. He didn't even have the "cuteness" of youth. He wasn't tough-looking nor was he sweet-looking. He was just boy—thin, pallid, angry.

The hill upon which our 215-acre farm is built was green from the winter rains. Jim received without comment my little travelogue. "There's the football field. That's the laundry and over there's the dairy. The boys do all the work, you know. It's a self-help system."

I took him to one of the five cottages where the boys live and introduced him to his "Granny"—his housemother—and then he slipped into the stream of routine living.

During the next weeks I waited for reports on him, but nothing of any significance was ever registered. If I asked his chaplain or counselor how Jim was faring, the reply would be a noncommittal one.

"Patterson? Very quiet boy. No. Nothing in particular to report."

It was strange how Jim Patterson gnawed at me. I thought I knew boys, but this one—was he a time bomb who had to explode one day?

The Republic's most important industry—for one frantic month it absorbs us almost totally—is the making of Christmas wreaths. It started as a hobby with our founder, Margaret Fowler, and then, during a period of great financial need, the boys began to make them in quantity for sale. Today it is a giant enterprise that saves us from having to make mail appeals for money.

Throughout the year the boys go out on field trips to gather leaves and cones and pods for these wreaths. When all the different ingredients have been gathered in, they are dried, drilled, wired, and finally stored in great bins until the last week in November. Then the redwood greenery comes down from the North and the Republic turns into a massive assembly line.

Each boy is given a free wreath to send out to whomever he chooses each year, and I noticed, as the wreath-making began, that Jim addressed his to the foster parents who had been so kind to him.

Then, at last, a counselor told me something unusual about Jim. "He says he wants to make some money."

Suddenly, I was concerned. What did Jim have in mind? The boys are given a very small allowance but when they want to make extra money they have to work extra hours. It's not easy, especially around wreath-time. I became fascinated by Jim's industry. He'd be up early at the dairy. At mealtimes he'd be in the kitchen washing dishes. Until late at night he'd load boxes at the government post-office set up for our Christmas rush.

I didn't learn what he was going to do with his extra money until the day before Christmas: I was talking to his housemother when Jim walked by. He was as silent and as unresponsive as ever.

"By the way," Mrs. Garnes whispered to me, "the mystery is solved. Jim used that money he worked for to buy a wreath."

"Another wreath!" I said, surprised and bewildered.

"Yes," she went on, "he sent it to his parents—his real parents, that is."

Time bomb? I had spent a year waiting for that boy to explode. There, talking to Mrs. Garnes, I almost wept. Jim Patterson had exploded all right, but in his own way, gently, with an act of goodness.

In the time he had been with us, this silent, deceptive-looking boy had learned everything we had tried to teach him about honesty and diligence and effort. But most of all he had mastered what perhaps is hardest for all men: to love people who do not love us.

Periodically we have a kind of graduation ceremony during which our boys receive their Republic citizenship certificates. The time came for Jim to "terminate," and I was heading out of my office on the way to the ceremonies when, to my amazement, I found him waiting for me in the hall. "Mr. Graves," he said.

"Yes, Jim."

"May I walk down the hall with you?"

"Sure," I nodded, and he fell into stride with me. Together we headed toward the assembly hall. I waited for him to say something, but he didn't. We walked the entire distance in silence. Then, we came to the door and both of us stopped. He turned and looked up at me.

His eyes still had that far away, lonely look, the same as the first time I saw him. But there was a difference. Now he was really trying to reach out to me.

"Well," he said, "so long, Mr. Graves." Then he stood back to let me enter.

In a way it was the most beautiful conversation I ever had.

The Lost Melody
by Norman Vincent Peale

At Christmastime I like to recall an old legend about the shepherds to whom the angels came. These men were sitting about their fire one evening, trying to remember the music that they had heard on the beautiful night of our Saviour's birth. The melody had been bright as a spring morning, sweet as the laughter of a child, but no one could sing or even hum it.

Suddenly, as they talked, they heard a faint bleating far up the hillside. At first no one moved. Each man knew that a lamb was in trouble, but the dangers of the darkness—the treacherousness of the rocky hillside or the chances of an encounter with wolves—held them frozen. Then, the youngest of the shepherds, little more than a boy, sprang to his feet and disappeared.

When he returned sometime later, he was bruised and bleeding from slipping among the jagged rocks. But he held a little lamb safely in his arms.

"The strangest thing happened!" the young shepherd said exultantly. "On the way back, for no reason that I know, music seemed to fill my mind."

And then, while the other shepherds gaped in awe, he sang to them the lost melody.

Years passed. The Babe born at Bethlehem grew to manhood and was known far and wide as a great prophet. One day, so the legend goes, His followers came to Him and said, "Master, there is a blind man who stops often at the gates, tells stories to children and sings a melody of great beauty. Won't You come and hear him?"

So Jesus went and listened to the sweetness of the blind man's song. Then, gently, Jesus touched His finger to the man's eyes.

The singer leaped to his feet, crying, "I see. I see again!" And looking upon Jesus, he asked in wonder, "Who are you?"

Jesus must have smiled. "We have met before—long ago. Do you remember when you first heard that melody?"

Then the man told Jesus about the night he rescued the little lamb.

"Yes," replied the Master. "It is given to many men to hear that refrain from My Father's choir; but all too few learn to keep it alive, as you have done, with a loving heart and kindly deeds."

I WOULD LIGHT A CANDLE

This Christmas I would light a candle
In some forlorn child's eye,
Place a new star of friendship
In someone's lonely skies.
I would put a sparkling wreath of joy
Where it might melt a bitter heart;
Be steadfast in my prayer for peace
For all the world, not just a part.
So in this season, love-beguiled,
Would I gift the little Christ Child.

Elizabeth Searle Lamb

> "We thought we were doing the giving that
> Christmas but learned otherwise."

Surprise Ending
by Irene B. Harrell

I turned up the fur collar of my coat against a near-freezing wind as I stepped from our warm station wagon into the bare dirt of a front yard on the outskirts of town. Our adult Sunday school class had chosen the address from a Salvation Army list in the evening paper and my husband and I had driven out to meet the family. The idea was to find out their immediate needs so that we could provide a merry Christmas for them, and then, more important, to work with them throughout the year to try to make a real difference, a Christian difference, in their lives.

We had asked God to guide us to the right family, but now it looked as though the house we had chosen was going to be empty. No smoke came from the chimney and in the front door there was only a hole where a knob and a lock might have been, once. But when we knocked, the rag of curtain at the window moved and a small face peered out. A minute passed and then the door was opened by a boy about eight years old.

"Hello," I said. "Is your mother home?"

"Mama not home," he announced gravely. "She workin'."

"Well, ah—is any grownup here with you?" He shook his head.

"Let's step in for a minute," my husband suggested. "The house'll get cold with the door standing open." The boy moved shyly back and we entered the tiny room.

I'll never forget what we saw. There was a bed, sagging to the floor, the mattress oozing stuffing at every rip and seam. No sheets, no blankets. A small chest of drawers in the corner held a dusty glass punch bowl with cups hanging around the rim. A Bible lay beside it. On the floor a chipped enamel pan held some lumps of corn meal mush the children had been eating by fistfuls. The black wood stove was icy cold.

The boy who had let us in now stood protectively between two smaller children, a boy and a girl. Her oversized slacks were held together by a safety pin. All three youngsters were barefoot.

And there was a baby. He was lying on a pile of straw and rags that had once been an upholstered chair. He was wearing a remnant of an undershirt and a diaper that hadn't been changed for a long time.

I thought of my own warmly dressed children and my baby in her lovely birch crib with its clean white sheets and I started to cry. I'd never really seen poverty before.

That afternoon we went back with blankets, shoes, diapers, food and clothes. Again, the mother was not there. But apparently she'd been home long enough to build a blazing fire, so hot the children had the front door standing wide open. A coal scuttle held scraps of linoleum from a pile of debris in the yard next door.

The next day we finally found the mother at home. Her name was Virginia and the children, in order of age, were Arthur Lee, Violet, Danny and the baby, David Ray. Virginia was a tiny woman in a yellow bouffant-organdy dress. She answered our questions quietly and was not offended that we had come to help.

What did she need most? A refrigerator so the baby's milk wouldn't sour, and something for the stove that wouldn't burn as fast as linoleum. . . .

The class found a refrigerator, a bed, a crib, several chairs, sheets, more blankets. On Christmas, there were toys for the children and clothes and food for everyone. The wood stove was replaced by an oil heater that would not go out while the mother was away. The class pledged the money to pay the oil bills for the coming year.

The family's immediate physical needs had been relatively easy to satisfy. But what about the Christian difference?

Every week or two my husband and I would go to see Virginia and her family. Sometimes we'd carry hand-me-downs, or groceries, or books, sometimes we'd go empty-handed, just to visit. But she always gave us the same warm greeting. I remember the pride with which she invited me to sit down. She hadn't been able to exercise that kind of courtesy before, when she had no chairs.

Frequently, our four older children went along with us on these visits, and occasionally we took the baby. I had to explain to Virginia about our baby. German measles during my pregnancy had left little Marguerite deaf. When I told Virginia that the doctors said nothing could be done about it, I could see she was deeply affected.

On our next visit she greeted us with shining eyes. "Oh, Mrs. Harrell," she said, "I believe God is going to make your baby hear! Don't you feel it too? Can't she already hear a lot better than she could? I've been praying so hard ever since you told me. I *know* she's going to hear!"

I just smiled at Virginia. She didn't know as much about science as I did. I couldn't expect her to understand that nerve deafness was not curable. Of course *I* had prayed for my child; but my prayers had been ones of thankfulness for her, not prayers for healing. I took the doctors' words as final.

Marguerite was almost a year old when we first noticed the change in her. For a while we couldn't believe it ourselves, but at last we became convinced that she really was hearing certain loud sounds. When we took her back to the hearing clinic for testing, there was no doubt about it. Our daughter, whose nerve deafness had been pronounced complete and incurable, had begun to hear! In four short months her diagnosis had changed from "profoundly deaf" to "moderately to severely hard of hearing."

The doctors were amazed, but Virginia wasn't even surprised. "God did it, Mrs. Harrell. Didn't I ask Him for an icebox and a good stove, and didn't He give them to me? There's nothing He can't do, if we just ask Him."

I stared at her, trying to understand faith like this, reaching out my own feeble portion to try to take hold of hers.

"Mrs. Harrell," she said, "I'm going to keep on praying for that baby."

"Yes!" I whispered, "Please keep praying. Don't ever stop."

It worked, you see, our Christmas project; it even accomplished the "Christian difference." Of course, the difference was in our lives, not Virginia's. But then, we'd asked God to guide us to the poor, and He generally knows where they are.

Section III
Christmas—A Time for Patience

Christmas is a time for patience,
When we try anew to mold
Our lives in the image of Him
Whose birthday we uphold.

Newlyweds Mike and Linda make
a discovery their first Christmas together.

The Christmas Everything Went Wrong
by Michael Suscavage

On December 25, 1968, we had been married exactly 26 days.
Linda and I had looked forward to our first Christmas in that
special, exciting way that turned everything we did together into
an historic first. It was as though we were consciously creating
and storing up memories, and we wanted this Christmas to be as
perfect as possible.

It was Linda's idea that we invite my parents to come into
New York from New Jersey for Christmas dinner at our apartment. They needed a change of scene, she reasoned, since I, of
course, was so recently married and my brother Wayne would
not be able to be home for the holidays; Wayne was in Vietnam.
We insisted they come in spite of the difficulties we knew we
faced.

There was our apartment, for instance. *Some* apartment! A
not-large living room, a not-large bedroom, a microscopic kitch-
en, a sprinkling of handsome wedding gifts and a few peculiari-
ties of furniture. For this honeymoon palace we paid a sum of
money that would keep us constantly broke, but it was located
on the convenient and nice East Side of Manhattan, exactly
where we wanted to live. We felt it worth our scrimping.

"Your mother and dad understand our apartment," Linda
said. "I'll work my wiles on a turkey. We have plenty of china
and silver, and I'll go out and find the best-looking Christmas
tree in town. We'll have this place looking more Christmasy than
the North Pole. It will be a Christmas to remember."

Her enthusiasm had convinced me.

But we had not counted on Linda's getting an assignment.
She's an airline stewardess, and though she was not originally
scheduled to fly Christmas Eve, there was a sudden call for her
that morning that sent her scurrying out of the house for a flight

to Denver. And neither of us counted on Dan Sawyer, my roommate from bachelor days, who, on the afternoon of Christmas Eve, told me he couldn't make it back to his folks in Syracuse. What else could I do but ask him to come spend Christmas with us?

So it was that Dan came home with me from my office Christmas Eve. "Meet the Christmas tree my dear wife paid twenty dollars for," I said to him as we forced our way into the apartment. All eight feet of the homely pine lay lifeless in the narrow hallway as if it had been hacked to the ground on that very spot. I was not disposed to liking that tree. Its needles now littered the room, and already it had managed to insinuate itself as an argument between Linda and me. Linda, I felt, had gone hog-wild on that monstrosity—a "bargain" for such a "beauty" at New York prices, or so she had told me. Even so, she knew full well how carefully we were supposed to be watching every penny. I was genuinely angry at her extravagance.

"We can't just leave it there," Danny said hours later as we sat staring at the tree. Ever since we arrived home it had been a stumbling block as we went back and forth to the refrigerator, rummaging for food and drink. "I think we'd better set it up."

"With what?" I asked. "We have no stand, no decorations and, thanks to Linda, no extra money."

Danny insisted we do something. Finally we succeeded in propping up the tree with our brand-new encyclopedia and, for security, nudging the monster against the wall. It was a pathetic sight.

That superhuman task completed, we relaxed. We talked. We mused about past Christmases, about all the preparations that used to keep our homes abuzz. Danny remembered, too, how efficient my mother had always been—the gifts carefully wrapped and set aside, the tree meticulously decorated, the meals fabulously planned.

Danny and I sat there in that drab room. From the couch I could look into the bedroom and see the pictureless walls and the sheets Linda and I had hung over the windows in lieu of curtains. And when I looked over at that bare Christmas tree, I felt just a little forlorn myself.

It must have been after midnight when the door buzzer shattered the melancholy. In no time the red and green of a very familiar airline uniform appeared in the room. Linda was home earlier than expected! But she was tired. Her eyes seemed to reflect overwork, and her long blond hair fell colorlessly to her weary shoulders. She gave me a tiny kiss and, if disappointed at seeing poor old Danny there, she didn't really show it. Then the tree caught her eye.

"The tree! The tree! You put it up!" She stood back to appraise it. "Ah, such *character*," she said in total approval, as a kind of twinkle returned to her. "You see, it *was* twenty dollars well spent. It transforms the room." Danny and I just looked at each other.

"Did you find the cranberries and popcorn?" she asked, turning to the kitchen. It was the first I had heard about them. "Good—you waited for me. We'll fix them and string them for the tree and cut out papers stars."

Linda darted into the kitchen and for the next several hours rattled and clanged and mumbled as she struggled to thaw and then stuff a half-frozen turkey. I proved inept at stringing cranberries, partly because the sewing needle Linda suggested I use was too small for the string she suggested I use. We never learned how to pop the corn properly. And the master of the paper-star department, Danny, wielded his scissors clumsily. In fact, more than anything, Danny was in the way. Annoyed, I said to him, "Just forget the stars." A smile could not hide his disappointment nor mask the flush in his face.

At 3:30 a.m. we called it quits. We all knew what a fiasco it had been. I blamed myself for having been angry about the cost of the tree, and for having been so helpless. And now I felt additionally helpless; I didn't know what I could do for Linda, who had tried so hard with so little to show for it. She made up the couch for our guest. The only good moment of the whole Christmas Eve came as I was closing our bedroom door and saw Danny in the living room, squatting before the Christmas tree, placing two little packages beneath its bare branches.

Too early in the morning Linda was up putting the turkey in the oven. Somehow the three of us stumbled off to an early church service and when we came back, we were so tired that we all went back to bed. Linda set the alarm, but it didn't go off. The extra rest was good for us, but not for the bird in the oven. Linda was distraught. Christmas dinner, she said, was "ruined." I didn't know what to say; I didn't know how to comfort her.

And at just that terrible moment, my family arrived: Mother

and Dad, their arms filled with packages, and to my surprise, Virginia, my brother Wayne's wife, was with them, her arms filled too. Not all of those packages were Christmas gifts. As though psychic, Mother had brought jars of her summer canning, some special pastries, a Christmas letter to us from Wayne, a large supply of her famous salad and dozens of the family Christmas-tree ornaments I recognized immediately. "I made a mince pie too, dear," Mother said to Linda, "but I burned it to a crisp."

Hearing about the mince pie had a strange and happy effect on Linda. "Have you ever had charcoal turkey?" Linda asked Mom, all twinkling again as the two of them disappeared, if I may use the expression, into the kitchen.

The turkey was dry all right, but surprisingly tasty. We marveled at it, and joked. And that was the tenor of the day. That was the way the day eased on. We sat at our makeshift dining table with our beautiful wedding china and crystal, and we enjoyed just being there together. At one special point, we remembered Wayne. My father led us in a prayer for his safe return and for peace everywhere. It was an appropriate ending for a lovely and loving day.

After everyone had gone, Linda and I sat together in what was now a very cluttered room, before a very beautiful tree. Linda said, "I think I understand when Christmas is most perfect— when *things* are most imperfect. Then people begin to depend on each other."

Linda was right. The more important we make things, the less important people become. We can work for, and hope for, a "perfect" Christmas, but the more we are caught up in engineering it, the more readily its mystery eludes us. Christmas is Christ's day, not our day, but He has a way of sharing it with us as we share with one another.

May We Keep It in Our Hearts
by Peter Marshall

In a world that seems not only to be changing, but even to be
dissolving, there are some tens of millions of us who want
Christmas to be the same . . .
>   with the same old greeting "Merry Christmas" and no other.
We long for the abiding love among men of good will which
>   the season brings . . .
believing in this ancient miracle of Christmas with its softening,
sweetening influence to tug at our heart strings once again.
We want to hold on to the old customs and traditions
because they strengthen our family ties,
>   bind us to our friends,
>   make us one with all mankind
for whom the Child was born,
and bring us back again to the God Who gave
His only begotten Son,
that "whosoever believeth in Him
should not perish, but have everlasting life."
So we will not "spend" Christmas . . .
>   nor "observe" Christmas.
We will "keep" Christmas—keep it as it is . . .
>   in all the loveliness
>   of its ancient traditions.
May we keep it in our hearts,
that we may be kept in its hope.

What can a family do when a dark
shadow falls across Christmas?

The Dime Store Angel
by Barbara Estelle Shepherd

When our twin daughters were toddlers and Scotty was still a
baby, my husband, Dick, and I dug into our meager Christmas
fund to buy a dime store angel for the top of our tree. Esthetical-
ly, she was no prize: the plastic wings were lopsided, the gaudy
robes painted haphazardly, the reds splashing over into the blues
and purples. At night, though, she underwent a mysterious
change—the light glowing from inside her robes softened the
colors and her golden hair shone with the aura of a halo.

For six years she had the place of honor at the top of our tree.
For six years, as in most families, Christmas was a time to be
especially grateful for the wonderful gifts of God.

And then, in the seventh year, as summer enfolded us in her
warm lethargy, I became aware of a new life gently stirring
beneath my heart. Of all God's gifts this seemed the culmina-
tion, for we had long prayed for another child. I came home
from the doctor's office and plunged straight into plans for a
mood-setting dinner.

That evening when Dick walked in, candles flickered on the
table and the children took their places, self-conscious in Sunday
clothes "when it's just Wednesday!"

"Oh-oh," he grinned, "Mother's up to something—one of
those special dinners again." I smiled and waited till halfway
through the meal to make the announcement. But I got no further
than the first informative sentence.

"You mean we're gonna have a baby?" squealed Miriam.
Milk overturned and chairs clattered. Doors slammed and Dick
and I were alone with our happiness while our three small Paul
Reveres galloped wildly over the neighborhood shouting their
news to everyone within lung distance.

Summer and fall sped by as we turned the spare room into a

nursery and scraped and repainted baby furniture. December came again; once more we were on the verge of Christmas. Then one morning, eight weeks too soon for our new nursery to be occupied, I was rushed to the hospital.

Shortly past noon our four-pound son was born. Still groggy from the anesthetic, I was wheeled—bed and all—to the nursery to view Kirk Steven through an incubator porthole. Dick silently squeezed my hand while we absorbed the doctor's account of the dangers Kirk would have to overcome in order to survive. Added to his prematurity was the urgency for a complete blood exchange to offset RH problems.

All that long afternoon Dick and I prayed desperately that our son's life be spared. It was evening when I awoke from an uneasy doze to find our minister standing by the bed. No word was spoken, but as he clasped my hand, I knew. Our little boy had lived less than 12 hours.

During the rest of that week in the hospital, grief and disbelief swept over me by turn. At last Dick came to take me home. He loaded my arms with a huge bouquet of red roses, but flowers can never fill arms that ache to hold a baby.

In the street outside I was astonished to see signs of Christmas everywhere: the decorated stores, the hurrying shoppers, the lights strung from every lamp post. I had forgotten the season. For the sake of the children at home, we agreed, we would go through the motions. But it would be no more than that.

And so a few days later Dick bought a tree and mechanically I joined him and the children in draping tinsel and hanging glass balls from the branches. Last of all, on the very top, went the forlorn dime store angel. Then Dick flipped the switch and again she was beautiful. Scotty gazed upward for a moment, then said softly, "Daddy, this year we have a *real* angel, don't we? The one God gave us."

And Dick and I, in our poverty, were going to give Christmas to our children—forgetting that it is always we who receive it from them! For, of course, God was the reality in tragedy as He had been in our joys, the unchanging Joy at the heart of all things. Scotty's words were for me like the light streaming now from the plastic angel, transforming what was poor and ugly on the surface into glory.

At five a.m. December 25 in Covington, Georgia,
Christmas and disaster collided.

Tornado!
by Charlotte Hale Smith

On the day before Christmas two years ago, the pastures of River
Bend Farm near Covington, Georgia, were lush-green with
winter rye grass. There, lording castle-like over 700 neat acres,
was the dairy barn, two-stories high and large enough for the
herd of 65 Holsteins on the ground floor, tons of stored hay and
feed on the second. This was what River Bend Farm was like on
the day before Christmas. On Christmas morning, the rye grass
was still lush-green, but there was no barn; there was little left of
the herd of Holsteins.

On the night which remembers Christ's birth, a ghostly tornado swirled through the Georgia countryside delivering not birth
but destruction and death. The tornado was ghostly because no
one at River Bend Farm saw it or felt its true havoc.

At five a.m. that Christmas morning, the Polk brothers, J. T.
Jr. and Charles, started out in their pick-up truck for their
morning chores. The Polks, who owned River Bend Farm, were
progressive farmers. They were much respected in the area as
good men and as good farmers. Over the years they had
improved their land, and their herd had maintained one of the
best production and quality records in the state. Both men—the
very tall, tanned, laconic J. T. and the younger, smaller, boyish
and fast-moving Charles—had a love for farming. This love
showed itself in unexpected ways, like the affectionate names
they had for each one of their many cows.

But this morning they sensed that something was wrong. It
was still dark; the morning was unusually warm; the fog, thick as
cream.

"Look, Charlie, last night's wind tore down the fence," J. T.
said.

"Electric line's down too," Charles said, alarmed. "Get a flashlight and help me find the cows."

Then they heard the lowing in the distance; deep, frightened sounds of distress. The brothers dashed through the fog only to stop, unbelieving. What had been an enormous barn was now a grotesquely flattened mass of splintered wood.

"The cows! Look for the cows!" J. T. yelled as he lunged off toward the pasture, hoping the animals hadn't escaped through the broken fence.

It was Charles who recognized the worst. "Come back, J. T.," he screamed. "The cows are *in* the barn!"

They didn't stop to think. They rushed in and started pulling bales of hay off the cows which were still alive. Other cows lay dead, twisted and crushed beneath the wreckage, suffocated by the 200 tons of hay that had fallen on them.

Once the brothers recognized the impossible task that faced them, they ran to the milking barn, called Civil Defense authorities, then raced back to their animals.

And soon, help came. Neighbors. Trucks. The implement company in nearby Covington sent two bulldozers; a neighbor arrived with a third. By daybreak the pastures and drives swarmed with people. Some came to watch, most stayed to work. When the Polks' driveway filled with trucks and machinery, friends cut the barbed wire to make new access. A State patrolman assumed traffic duty.

By afternoon, J. T. and Charles were in a daze, but they and nearly a hundred volunteers kept working, forgetting their Christmas stockings and the turkeys that would have to go in the ovens another day. The bulldozers dug in and pushed the debris aside, veterinarians ministered to injured animals, farmers loaded salvaged hay onto waiting trucks. The town's two hardware stores opened and distributed work gloves, pitchforks and shovels. Someone drove a haybaler to the scene and men retrieved scattered hay, rebaled it, loaded it aboard trucks.

By nightfall, River Bend Farm was neat again; there was a foundation dug and ready for a new barn. Exhausted, indescribably grateful, the brothers went home. Grateful they were, but beaten down. They had lost 47 cows. They faced a desperate future.

But the Polks had not reckoned fully with their neighbors. The community rallied even after Christmas had passed. They started bringing cows, one or two at a time, as gifts from farmers nearby and across the state. Mennonite farmers from Montezuma, Georgia—men utterly unknown to Covington farmers—brought 13 Holsteins, all top-quality milk cows, all gifts. And a fine Holstein costs $350 or more.

Other people gave money. Friends contributed $50, $100; one man gave $1,000. Fellow dairymen raised nearly $4,000 and there were people they didn't know who sent smaller sums from far across the United States.

Good deeds multiplied. A farm equipment firm replaced ruined implements at cost. Farmers donated feed, neighbors helped raise a new barn from materials donated or bought at cost and the building contractor gave his skills.

The Polks' wives wrote thank-you letters to as many people as they could, then worried because they couldn't track down everyone who helped.

Within six weeks, River Bend Farm had resumed operations, falteringly. By spring, new calves frisked in the pastures, and by summer the farm had begun to beat its own production records.

Christmas. It is returning again as it does every year, as it does everywhere, finding people in sorrow, in joy, in the emptiness or fullness of life. It is finding no one the same as the year before. The Polks this year are different from the year of the tornado. They are better for their neighbors; they have been filled with the meaning of brotherhood, the meaning which so much of the world forgets—or refuses to remember.

One of America's best-loved novelists
tells the story of her most memorable Christmas.

My Christmas Miracle
by Taylor Caldwell

For many of us, one Christmas stands out from all the others, the one when the meaning of the day shone clearest.

Although I did not guess it, my own "truest" Christmas began on a rainy spring day in the bleakest year of my life. Recently divorced, I was in my 20s, had no job, and was on my way downtown to go the rounds of the employment offices. I had no umbrella, for my old one had fallen apart, and I could not afford another one. I sat down in the streetcar, and there against the seat was a beautiful silk umbrella with a silver handle inlaid with gold and flecks of bright enamel. I had never seen anything so lovely.

I examined the handle and saw a name engraved among the golden scrolls. The usual procedure would have been to turn in the umbrella to the conductor, but on impulse I decided to take it with me and find the owner myself. I got off the streetcar in a downpour and thankfully opened the umbrella to protect myself. Then I searched a telephone book for the name on the umbrella and found it. I called, and a lady answered.

Yes, she said in surprise, that was her umbrella, which her parents, now dead, had given her for a birthday present. But, she added, it had been stolen from her locker at school (she was a teacher) more than a year before. She was so excited that I forgot I was looking for a job and went directly to her small house. She took the umbrella, and her eyes filled with tears.

The teacher wanted to give me a reward, but—though $20 was all I had in the world—her happiness at retrieving this special possession was such that to have accepted money would have spoiled something. We talked for a while, and I must have given her my address. I don't remember.

The next six months were wretched. I was able to obtain only temporary employment here and there, for a small salary, though this was what they now call the Roaring Twenties. But I put aside 25 or 50 cents when I could afford it for my little girl's Christmas presents. (It took me six months to save $8.) My last job ended the day before Christmas, my $30 rent was soon due, and I had $15 to my name—which Peggy and I would need for food. She was home from her convent boarding school and was excitedly looking forward to her gifts the next day, which I had already purchased. I had bought her a small tree, and we were going to decorate it that night.

The stormy air was full of the sound of Christmas merriment as I walked from the streetcar to my small apartment. Bells rang and children shouted in the bitter dusk of the evening, and windows were lighted and everyone was running and laughing. But there would be no Christmas for me, I knew, no gifts, no remembrance whatsoever. As I struggled through the snowdrifts, I just about reached the lowest point in my life. Unless a miracle happened I would be homeless in January, foodless, jobless. I had prayed steadily for weeks, and there had been no answer but this coldness and darkness, this harsh air, this abandonment. God and men had completely forgotten me. I felt old as death, and as lonely. What was to become of us?

I looked in my mailbox. There were only bills in it, a sheaf of them, and two white envelopes which I was sure contained more bills. I went up three dusty flights of stairs, and I cried, shivering in my thin coat. But I made myself smile so I could greet my little daughter with a pretense of happiness. She opened the door for me and threw herself in my arms, screaming joyously and demanding that we decorate the tree immediately.

Peggy was not yet six years old, and had been alone all day while I worked. She had set our kitchen table for our evening meal, proudly, and put pans out and the three cans of food which would be our dinner. For some reason, when I looked at those pans and cans, I felt brokenhearted. We would have only hamburgers for our Christmas dinner tomorrow, and gelatin. I stood in the cold little kitchen, and misery overwhelmed me. For the first time in my life, I doubted the existence of God and His mercy, and the coldness in my heart was colder than ice.

The doorbell rang, and Peggy ran fleetly to answer it, calling that it must be Santa Claus. Then I heard a man talking heartily to her and went to the door. He was a delivery man, and his arms were full of big parcels, and he was laughing at my child's frenzied joy and her dancing. "This is a mistake," I said, but he read the name on the parcels, and they were for me. When he had gone I could only stare at the boxes. Peggy and I sat on the floor and opened them. A huge doll, three times the size of the one I had bought for her. Gloves. Candy. A beautiful leather purse. Incredible! I looked for the name of the sender. It was the teacher, the address simply "California," where she had moved.

Our dinner that night was the most delicious I had ever eaten. I could only pray in myself, "Thank You, Father." I forgot I had no money for the rent and only $15 in my purse and no job. My child and I ate and laughed together in happiness. Then we decorated the little tree and marveled at it. I put Peggy to bed and set up her gifts around the tree, and a sweet peace flooded me like a benediction. I had some hope again. I could even examine the sheaf of bills without cringing. Then I opened the two white envelopes. One contained a check for $30 from a company I had worked for briefly in the summer. It was, said a note, my "Christmas bonus." My rent!

The other envelope was an offer of a permanent position with the government—to begin two days after Christmas. I sat with the letter in my hand and the check on the table before me, and I think that was the most joyful moment of my life up to that time.

The church bells began to ring. I hurriedly looked at my child, who was sleeping blissfully, and ran down to the street. Everywhere people were walking to church to celebrate the birth of the Saviour. People smiled at me and I smiled back. The storm had stopped, the sky was pure and glittering with stars.

"The Lord is born!" sang the bells to the crystal night and the laughing darkness. Someone began to sing, "Come, all ye faithful!" I joined in and sang with the strangers all about me.

I am not alone at all, I thought. *I was never alone at all.*

And that, of course, is the message of Christmas. We are never alone. Not when the night is darkest, the wind coldest, the world seemingly most indifferent. For this is still the time God chooses.

THE MIRACLE OF CHRISTMAS

The wonderment
  in a small child's eyes,
The ageless awe
  in the Christmas skies . . .
The nameless joy
  that fills the air,
The throngs that kneel
  in praise and prayer . . .
These are the things
  that make us know
That men may come
  and men may go,
But none will
  ever find a way
To banish Christ
  From Christmas Day . . .
For with each child
  there's born again
A Mystery that baffles men.

Helen Steiner Rice

It isn't a time to feel sorry for yourself,
they found, but a time to rejoice.

The Loneliest Christmas Until. . . .

by Helen G. Baer

For the first time in my life I dreaded the approach of the
Christmas season. We would be lonely, my husband and I. This
was the first Christmas since our two daughters had married and
set up homes of their own; the first, too, that Mother, with her
gift of sharing happiness with others, would not be with us.
Always before, December had found our house up to the eaves in
colored paper, gifts and secrets. Now it was orderly and forlorn.

"It doesn't seem worthwhile getting a tree this year, does it,
dear?" I said to my husband as we sat together after dinner one
evening.

"We aren't the first ones to have kids grow up," he said
briskly. "If we think we're going to be lonely, let's find some
other folks to share Christmas with."

I pondered what he said all evening and the next morning I
telephoned an elderly couple whose son was out of the country
on business, inviting them to supper on Christmas Eve.

"Of course, we'll come," the old lady said with a catch in
her voice.

A little later I recalled having met a young Japanese couple,
new citizens. They joyfully accepted my invitation to our tree-
trimming. Only then did I realize that we were to have a tree
after all. Out of the blue, a friend telephoned to inquire if we
would entertain some foreign students during the holidays. "How
about Christmas Eve?" I asked. It was arranged that three
Japanese exchange students would join us.

The night before, Christmas had looked like a lonely thing.
Suddenly we had seven guests. I scurried to find small gifts for
them, to make the pudding, to decorate the house.

In the midst of the scramble, the telephone rang again. It was the old lady. Her son had returned unexpectedly. Might they bring him?

"But of course!"

Our party seemed to snowball.

Somehow we heard of a hospital intern far from home who would have no Christmas unless we took him in too, and then a letter arrived from a German girl whose father was a business associate of my husband. She had school permission to come to us if we would have her. Our table count was up to 12!

But we hadn't reckoned with our girls. The phone rang still another time. "Mother," I heard my older daughter say, "we've talked it over and we want Christmas Eve with you and Dad. We'll do our own trees beforehand, but we want to be with you when the lights go on. Do you still have room for us?"

Had we room for them indeed. What parents ever did not have room for their very own?

If we'd been busy before, it was nothing to the activity now, cleaning, buying a tree, cooking. . . .

They arrived in midafternoon, those lonesome students, the old couple and their shy son, the young doctor who became at ease as soon as he saw the dimples of our pretty German house guest. Our Japanese friends came shortly before our children.

I spread the tree trimmings on the floor and everyone enthusiastically went to work.

When we finished, we turned off all but the tree lights and my husband brought out his banjo and we sang carols in whichever language each of us knew. *Silent Night* is as beautiful in Japanese as it is in German or English.

Then we started *Jingle Bells* as we handed out the packages and accepted the delightful tokens our friends had brought us from their native lands. Supper was a joyous event and after it each one told of some special Christmas memory. It was late when our guests left.

Our girls left last of all. "It wouldn't be Christmas anywhere but here," they said as they kissed us good night. We closed the door behind them and my husband put his arm around me. "Merry Christmas, darling," he said, and both of us knew that we had found Christmas once more, for Christmas was the love in our own hearts. I knew now that the season of Christ's birth isn't a time to feel sorry for oneself—it is a time to give of oneself.

How do you celebrate Christmas
in a hospital?

Yuletide Is Not Always So Merry
by Faith Baldwin

Once, not so long ago, I spent Christmas in a hospital, but not as
a patient. In Baltimore a child of mine had lain for several
months and would for many more to follow. We had resigned
ourselves to the fact that for the first time since their birth, all the
children of this household would not be together under their own
roof in Connecticut.

Always there has been a tree, and the stockings have been
hung and a great scurrying about the house has begun long
before the Eve. And for a number of years upon that Eve we
have gone to sing carols around a community tree and to church
afterwards and then home, where we put the gifts in their
appointed places, and then retired, all, even the oldest among us,
too excited to sleep. But this year would be different.

We said, "No tree at home. Only one, a little one in the
hospital room," and we were sensible, I think. But I am not
really sensible. I mourned in my heart, which was silly of me,
for I had known half a century's procession of lighted trees. Yet
it was not, you understand, the tree I was mourning. . . .

I think it was on December twenty-first—a tree came to our
home and was set up where it always stands. For those who
loved me had said to one another, "She shall have her tree. . . ."

So on that day, and that day only, for we would not see it
again, the tree was trimmed for me and the gifts brought down.
We opened them, those we had wrapped against this time,
thinking to open them long after December twenty-fifth had
come and gone. And we had a sort of special dinner; just three of
us, that evening, and said to one another "Merry Christmas."
We were not merry.

When we set off for Baltimore, we were laden with luggage
and boxes, with gifts for our little girl in the hospital; gifts which

included her first fur coat, gray and soft as a cloud. And we also brought small things for one another and our stockings to hang so that we might wake in the hotel on Christmas Day and feel somewhat at home.

I do not recall whether or not it snowed that year in that city: I think so, but am not sure. I have a remembrance of grayness and cold. But I remember most vividly the hospital room and the radiance of spirit within it, a spirit which transcended the long, brutal pain. The spirit shook me, because it was where I had not expected it.

We went shopping in that city, the child's godmother, her twin brother and I. We bought the fragile things for her tree which we could not bring with us; we bought garlands for her windows and a tree. . . .

There was a marble fireplace in that old fashioned room and we hung her stocking there, put the tree on the hearth, trimmed it, and set the wreaths in place and the gifts all about. And all the spirit that is Christmas laughed at us from the high hospital bed, with its ugly arrangement of ropes and pulleys and weights.

We left her at nine o'clock on Christmas Eve and returned to our hotel and hung our own stockings over the mantel in the impersonal living room and went to bed.

In the morning we had the small packages we had saved for this occasion and placed the long-distance telephone calls to those we missed and still could reach, and went to the hospital. And the tree had a special significance, as did the crammed stockings, the gay wreaths and bright paper wrappings.

I remember that later I went down the corridor from which many doors led to pain or death or slow returning life. I walked into a telephone booth, closed the door, but even through the glass I could hear the nurses laughing, and so I looked out and saw him—my tall boy walking down the corridor modelling his sister's fur coat. And I thought of all the people over all the many years who had sat in this same booth and spoken into the little black mouth of the telephone and of the things they had said, desperate things or hopeful; tragic things or happy . . . on holidays like this.

We ate our Christmas dinner in the hotel that afternoon. I remember only being astonished at the custom which I had encountered in that same dining room at Thanksgiving—of serving sauerkraut with turkey. Then we took two Christmas dinners to the hospital, complete in every respect, for our girl and her nurse.

But most of all I remember, that every time we entered or left the hospital we passed the gigantic, merciful figure of Christ with outstretched arms which stands there to bring to the anxious human heart the age-old assurance of life immortal and love enduring.

This was but one Christmas out of many. I recall the earliest in my memory; it seems to be a tiny picture of a tree, of a sugar plum and of a great phonograph with a morning glory horn and strange sounds issuing from the box, the wax cylinders turning and turning. I remember another Christmas, when sick for home, I stood in the brilliant sunlight of the sub-tropics and looked at the palm trees and longed for snow and firs and the Christmas fragrance . . . never stopping to think that the Child whose birthday we celebrate was born under bright skies and with the speaking palms nearby.

In many homes Christmas is something people wish to forget and cannot because of the symbols all about them; perhaps, at this season some one loved has slipped away. . . . Perhaps, they say, "I don't believe in Christmas." *Why?* For none has really gone from the house he once inhabited or from the hearts dedicated to him. And who does not "believe" in Christmas cannot believe in himself, for in each of us there abides the Spirit which *is* Christmas, the Spirit which is hope and joy and strength.

All one day not long ago I found myself thinking, "What is man, that Thou art mindful of him?" I awoke thinking this; I had slept with the question in my mind. Somehow, at Christmas it is given to us to know the answer. For whatever man is, or is not, he is created in his Maker's image and is by his Creator, loved, and forgiven.

I remember that years ago a friend sent me a war-time newspaper from New Zealand, telling of a group of refugees from torpedoed ships who were landed just before Christmas on a lonely island. I later wrote this story for one of the magazines; it was a true story about the wounded and the ill, about men, women and children, about fear and agony and loss. A story of heroism and humility. And a story of people who, from whatever means at hand, built an altar and robed their Priest in vestments of white calico and red twill procured at the native store, and who on the Eve of Christmas, carried lanterns through tropical groves heavy with fragrance, came, singing and marching to the altar, Catholic and Protestant alike, to celebrate the Mass and take Communion.

For Christmas can be celebrated everywhere; in a hospital room, under a palm tree, on a lost, lonely island and in the heart. For beyond the symbols and the tradition there is the Spirit, the year round Spirit . . . if we but seek its unfailing Source.

> She had gone to Korea to work in an orphanage—a
> starry-eyed volunteer. By Christmas the stars were gone.

The Failure That Helped Me Grow Up
by Penny Defore

with a few fond interruptions by her
actor-father Don Defore

It seems hard to believe that only two years ago I spent Christmas in a Korean orphanage. This was an experience I'll always remember.

Don DeFore speaking: *In this article, my 19-year-old daughter Penny tells the story of her 1960 trip to Korea as a starry-eyed teenager to work as a volunteer in an orphanage not far from Seoul. She tells it honestly and vividly, but modestly, I think. I suffer from no such bashfulness where Penny is concerned, and so with your permission I would like to break in occasionally with a comment of my own. All right, Penny, over to you....*

The first thing I was aware of on that bleak Christmas morning two years ago was cold: biting, bone-chilling cold. I was sleeping in most of my clothes, including a heavy fleece-lined parka. When I opened my eyes and looked around the bare little room where I slept alone—no electricity, no running water, no fireplace, no radiators—I couldn't help contrasting my surroundings with the warmth and luxury I had known on other Christmases.

Seven thousand miles away, I knew, my mother and my father and my four younger brothers and sisters would be thinking about me, missing me. When I thought of them, I could feel tears of homesickness sting my eyes.

I was an American teenager in a Korean orphanage, and I was there by choice. For four years—ever since I was 13—I had been hoping to go to Korea, planning to go, pleading with my parents to let me go. The reason was simple—or seemed simple to me. I had been given so much that I wanted to give something back.

All my life I had had everything a girl could want: a wonderful family, friends, comfort, security, love. I took these privileges completely for granted until the day in 1956 when I went to visit my father on a movie set and was introduced to a group of war orphans from Korea.

The picture they were making was *Battle Hymn,* a story based on the experiences of Col. Dean Hess of the U.S. Air Force who founded a home for Korean children orphaned by the war. About 25 of these children were in the film, and I was appalled by the hardships they had endured.

Don DeFore speaking: *Penny told us then that some day she wanted to go to Korea and try to help these unfortunate people. In the meantime, she said, she was going to raise money for the orphanage. She did too: by selling cakes and cookies and by working in the restaurant I then owned in Disneyland. In four years, Penny earned more than $700 for the orphanage.*

What was more, she said she had a feeling that God wanted her to go to Korea. Her mother and I tried to talk her out of it, but if a child wants to be unselfish, wants to give herself, wants to help others, how long can parents stand in the way? Finally we gave in. Worried? Of course we were worried! Sending a 17-year-old 7,000 miles would worry any parent!

Christmas Day was no time to be thinking about the cold, or my homesickness. I jumped up (believe me, I didn't have much dressing to do!), took my Bible in one hand and the little Santa Claus puppet an inspired friend had given me back in California, and ran down the path to the buildings where more than 250 orphans shivered in dormitories even colder than my room.

We had a happy Christmas morning together, those orphans and I. They loved it when I made the Santa Claus puppet bow and clap his hands for them; the language barrier was no problem for old Santa! We sang Christmas carols, and had a Christmas dinner that was somewhat better than the usual menu of rice, or seaweed wrapped in rice. For a little while the spirit of Christmas seemed to prevail. But as the freezing dusk began to settle, I felt terribly discouraged.

It wasn't just homesickness. It was something more frightening than that. It was a feeling that had been growing stronger ever since my arrival. The feeling that for all my good intentions, for all my desire to help, I really was not welcome. I was an outsider with alien ideas, with standards and attitudes that were different and therefore dangerous. The officials of the orphanage did not like it when I tried to help some of the children with their chores. They were incensed when I protested the harsh punishment given some of the children whose crime was selling the rags they wore in order to buy a pitiful taste of candy.

Don DeFore speaking: *Truth was, Penny had entered another world, a world where cruelty was common, where life was cheap, where standards of honesty and morality were different from our own. For the first time in her life, our Penny was face to face with the problem of evil . . . and she was facing it all alone.*

Perhaps it was a reaction to the emotionalism of Christmas, perhaps it was just self-pity, but when I finally went back to my little room I was overwhelmed with loneliness and despair. I tried to pray. All my life I have found peace of mind and renewed strength in prayer. Now I asked God to help me overcome the hostility I felt around me, to make me so understanding and loving that all the barriers would melt away.

And right there, in the middle of my prayer, came a thought so shattering and terrifying that I couldn't go on. It was the thought that perhaps this whole endeavor was not God's will for me at all, that it was nothing more than the romantic desire of a self-centered child who craved excitement and the publicity. *You're not really following God's plan for you,* a voice said inside of me. *You're following your own.*

That was the thought, the grim and desolate thought, with which I ended Christmas. I blew out the candle and crawled into bed, and I'm afraid my pillow was pretty damp before I finally fell asleep.

Don DeFore speaking: *It is a frightening thing to lose your conviction that what you're doing has God's approval. But many great souls have lived through such a crisis. And I, myself, believe that on that freezing Christmas night, in that far-off place, our Penny ceased to be a child and became that lonely, doubting, hesitant, groping thing: an adult human being.*

In the days that followed, I kept trying to do the things I had come to do. I began to learn a few words of Korean. I played with the children, sang songs to them, taught them games. They were wonderful: shy at first, then more and more responsive. But still I could not seem to break through the wall that separated me from the adult Koreans.

One night, praying about my situation, I told the Lord that I no longer knew whether it was His will for me to be in Korea or not. I told Him that no matter how I tried I could not seem to please the people in authority. I told Him that I was unable to cope with the problem any longer, and so I was turning it over to Him. If He wanted me to stay in Korea, I would stay. If He wanted me to go, I would go.

Three days later a visitor came to the orphanage. It was Dr. Kenneth Scott, a missionary who ran the Church World Service clinic for crippled children in Seoul. How much he knew about my situation, I don't know, but he asked me gently if I would like to transfer to his clinic, work as a therapist there, and live with some American friends of his in Seoul who had a daughter my age. I was so moved by this answer to my prayer that I was speechless. All I could do was nod my head.

The children wept when I left, and so did I. A failure? Yes, it was a failure. My brave hopes were disappointed. I had come up against a closed door, and I could not get through. But I believe God was trying to teach me something. He was trying to teach me that it isn't always enough to have good intentions and missionary zeal. You also must be prepared to suffer defeat.

And I learned another thing. When God closes one door for you, He often opens another. The months I spent in Korea after leaving the orphanage were joyous, happy, useful ones. The Scotts taught me how to put braces on the crippled children, how to help them eat, play games, walk with parallel bars. It was astounding, really: as soon as I surrendered my problem to God, I found myself doing what I had come to Korea to do.

I'm back in this wonderful country, now, but I'll never forget those two months I spent in the orphanage. Not only did they help me grow up, but they strengthened my faith in God's goodness and patience. If you just seek to do His will, He'll help you do it. That's the lesson I learned in Korea two years ago. It was the Christmas I'll never forget.

Don DeFore speaking: *Penny is in college now, studying to be a nurse. She hopes to go back to Korea, someday, with all the skill and training that she can acquire. She's not discouraged by what she calls her failure. To fail, and to learn, and to try again . . . that's what God wants us to do, isn't it? We think so, Penny, her mother and I.*

Christmas Is Always
by Dale Evans Rogers

Christmas was not just a starlit night in Bethlehem: it had been behind the stars forever.

There was Christmas in the heart of God when He made the earth, and then gave it away—to us. When He sent us His prophets, that was Christmas too. And it was the most magnificent Christmas of all, that night in Bethlehem when He gave us His own son.

As Jesus grew up, Christmas was everywhere He went, giving food, giving sight, giving life. For Christmas is giving.

But Christmas is also receiving. In the Bible it says: *As many as received Him, to them gave He power to become the sons of God* . . .

As many as received Him! When we understand that, we understand that receiving can be even more important than giving—at Christmas! When we receive Christ, we experience completely the gift that is Christmas.

Then, for us, Christmas is truly always, for Jesus said, *Lo, I am with you always* . . .

And Christmas is Jesus!

Section IV
Christmas—A Time for Giving

Christmas is a time for giving,
The Wise Men brought their best,
But Christ showed that the gift of self
Will out-give all the rest.

The best present is tied
with your heart strings.

Try Giving Yourself
by Arline Boucher and John Tehan

Gracious giving requires no special talent, nor large amounts of money. It is compounded of the heart and the head acting together toward the perfect means of expressing our feelings. It is love sharpened with imagination. For as Emerson explains, "The only gift is a portion of thyself."

To plan the gift of yourself does not take cleverness. But it requires a little more thought than you might ordinarily use, and far less dependency on the power of the dollar. A little girl whose pennies did not add up to enough for what she considered a suitable present for her mother, gave her several small boxes tied with bright ribbons. Inside each were slips of paper on which the child had printed, "Good for two flower-bed weedings," "Good for three batches of cookies for your bridge club," "Good for two floor scrubbings." She had never read Emerson, but unconsciously she put a large part of her small self into her gift.

When unexpected dental expense put a hole in a business girl's budget at Christmas, she hit upon a similar happy idea. Her presents that year were "time credit slips" upon which her friends could cash at their convenience. A couple with young children received slips entitling them to leave the baby with her for two weekends. To a niece in college went an offer of her car for a Christmas vacation trip. An elderly shut-in could claim her time for five reading sessions. A friend who loved to cook but who lived in a hotel was given a slip for the use of her apartment—and her stove—for an evening when she wanted to entertain. No costly present she had ever chosen had given her so much satisfaction—both ways—as these gifts of service.

Imagination was the chief ingredient in each of these gifts, as it was in the wedding present a young bride received from an

95

older woman. With it went a note, "Do not open 'til you and your husband have your first tiff." Many months passed until there came a day of not-so-sweet words and misunderstanding. In desperation the bride remembered the package. In it she found a card box filled with her friend's favorite recipes—and a note, "You will catch more flies with honey than you will with vinegar." It was a wise woman indeed, who gave of her experience with her gift.

A minister soliciting for a worthy cause was turned down by a well-to-do business man with a curt letter which ended, "As far as I can see, this Christian business is one continuous give, give, give." The clergyman wrote back, "Thank you for the best definition of the Christian life I have ever heard." Often the most successful gift is a spontaneous one. Act while the impulse is fresh. Take full advantage of the thrill of surprise—giving of yourself knows no special days.

Probably no gift ever thrilled a doctor more than a letter he received—out of the blue—from a youngster on *her* birthday. "Dear Doc, 14 years ago you brought me into this world. I want to thank you for I have enjoyed every minute of it."

Family gifts should be the easiest to anticipate because we know—or should know—each member's wish and whim. Yet how often we make the stereotyped offerings—ties, candy, or household utensils. One man I know is planning a present for his wife that will give them both pleasure for the rest of their lives. I saw him coming out of a dancing studio and kidded him about taking lessons. He admitted it and begged me not to tell a soul. "I got tired of hearing my wife complain about my dancing," he explained. "It's going to be a birthday present for her—my doing the samba!" An elderly lady on an Iowa farm wept with delight when her son in New York had a telephone installed in her house, and followed it up with a weekly long distance call.

Flowers brighten the hospital room and cheer the patient. They are our first thought for a sick friend. Too rarely do we progress beyond it to a second, more imaginative idea—to the gift that silently urges the patient to get well and use it.

"Over here is the sort of thing I'd like to have sent someone myself," a man in the hospital ward pointed out. It was an ordinary flower pot filled with dirt. On top was a packet of mixed seeds with the note, "You'll have more fun growing your own!" A nurse told me about a woman patient whose recovery dated from the moment a neighbor brought her an aluminum pressure cooker, something she had always wanted.

In her autobiography, *His Eye is on the Sparrow*, Ethel Waters tells about her gift to writer Rex Stout when he was convalescing. Though she was starring at the time in a Broadway play, she turned up early one morning at the hospital and, dressed as a nurse, she carried in his breakfast tray. She spent the day with Stout, diverting him with chitchat, wheeling his chair, giving him all her attention. Friends of the author said that this was his most cherished gift.

In your own profession, business or hobby you have gift opportunities that others do not have. On Christmas morning, a woman waiting for a trolley to go to the station in Washington, D.C., was surprised when a taxi skidded to a stop beside her. The driver motioned her to get in. At the station when she fumbled for her purse for the fare, the driver laughed and said, "Nothing doing—I asked you. Merry Christmas." In memory of her sister who was killed in service during the war, a waitress often pays the checks of servicewomen who sit at her table. She doesn't tell them whose guests they are. The widow of a college president took a clerical job to support herself so that she could give her husband's estate untouched to the college for a scholarship fund "for boys who love learning as much as my husband did."

All gifts that contain a portion of self, say that someone has been thinking of us, watching us, learning us by heart. It must have been a big Christmas for one sailor's mother when she opened her gift. At the Ships' Service store when he bought the most expensive engagement ring, the clerk asked him if he expected to get married soon. The sailor replied, "No, this is for my mother. She never owned a diamond in her life—and she had a lot of trouble bringing me up."

One of the most useful and thoughtful travel presents a girl ever received was currency of the country to which she was going. It was Mexico, and from a bank handling foreign coinage a friend had bought some one and five peso coins and some ten and 20 peso notes. Such a gift meant that she would have the correct money for tips and taxi fare when she first arrived.

Money, however, can be the touchiest gift to give graciously, especially when you know the person needs it. A young man realized that his visit with a retired couple of limited means could not help but put a dent in their budget. Offering to share food expenses was out of the question. So with his thank you note the guest included a ten dollar bill and added this postscript, "I happened to run across this fine miniature of Alexander Hamilton and thought you might like to add it to your collection." The response came back, "We thank you for that reproduction of the Hamilton engraving. It has been a long time since we have had the pleasure of viewing such a beautiful work of art. God bless you." This offering could not offend; the way in which it was given protected all concerned from embarrassment.

A GI stationed in Mississippi tells this story of a loan that became a gift. "I made friends with a share-cropper who lived near camp. Though poor, he was the most contented man I had ever met. One day when I was grousing about not being able to borrow $20 that I needed, the share-cropper handed me the money, saying it was a gift, not a loan. He explained it this way, 'If I loan you this money and for some reason you never return it, I must always think you have wronged me. If I give it to you as a gift, we're both happy—you because you received the gift and I because I gave. When you have the money and feel you want to make me a gift of $20, then we'll both be happy again—for the same reason.' "

The ultimate of selfless giving occurred recently at a service base hospital. In one ward lay an American soldier facing blindness, both of his eyes had been injured in a shrapnel explosion. Two beds away lay a sailor with an injured leg. When he learned of the soldier's plight, he insisted on giving the cornea of his right eye. "Then we'll both be able to see," he said. When the two men were rolled out to the operating room, the ward rocked with cheers.

Chances for such heroic giving are rare, yet every day there are opportunities to give a part of yourself to someone who needs it. It may be no more than a kind word or a letter written at the right time. It may be only a hand clasp. The important thing about any gift is the amount of yourself you put into it.

He gave his father something
neither would forget.

The Gift That Lasts a Lifetime
by Pearl S. Buck

We woke suddenly and completely. It was four o'clock, the hour at which his father had always called him to get up and help with the milking. Strange how the habits of his youth still clung to him after 50 years! He had trained himself to turn over and go to sleep, but this morning because it was Christmas, he did not try to sleep.

Yet what was the magic of Christmas now? His childhood and youth were long past, his father and mother were dead, and his own children grown up and gone. He and his wife were alone.

Yesterday she had said, "Let's not trim the tree until tomorrow, Robert—I'm tired."

He had agreed, and the tree was still out in the yard.

He slipped back in time, as he did so easily nowadays. He was 15 years old and still on his father's farm. He loved his father. He had not known how much until one day a few days before Christmas, when he had overheard what his father was saying to his mother.

"Mary, I hate to call Rob in the mornings. He's growing so fast and he needs his sleep. I wish I could manage alone."

"Well, you can't, Adam." His mother's voice was brisk.

"I know," his father said slowly, "but I sure do hate to wake him."

When he heard these words, something in him woke: his father loved him! He had never thought of it before. He got up quicker after that, stumbling blind with sleep, and pulled on his clothes, his eyes tight shut, but he got up.

And then on the night before Christmas, that year when he was 15, he lay on his side and looked out of his attic window. He wished he had a better present for his father than a ten-cent store tie.

The stars were bright outside, and one star in particular was so bright that he wondered if it were really the Star of Bethlehem. "Dad," he had once asked, "what is a stable?"

"It's just a barn," his father had replied, "like ours."

Then Jesus had been born in a barn, and to a barn the shepherds and the Wise Men had come, bringing their Christmas gifts.

The thought struck him like a silver dagger. Why should he not give his father a special gift? He could get up early, earlier than four o'clock, and he could creep into the barn and get all the milking done. He'd do it alone—milk and clean up, and then when his father went in to start the milking, he'd see it all done. And he would know who had done it.

He must have waked 20 times during the night. At a quarter to three he got up and put on his clothes. He crept downstairs, careful of the creaky boards, and let himself out. A big star hung low over the barn roof, a reddish gold. The cows looked at him, sleepy and surprised.

He had never milked all alone before, but it seemed almost easy. He kept thinking about his father's surprise. He smiled and milked steadily, two strong streams rushing into the pail, frothing and fragrant. The cows were still surprised but acquiescent. For once they were behaving well, as though they knew it was Christmas.

The task went more easily than he had ever known it to before. Milking for once was not a chore. It was something else, a gift to his father who loved him.

Back in his room he had only a minute to pull off his clothes in the darkness and jump into bed, for he heard his father up. He put the covers over his head to silence his quick breathing. The door opened.

"Rob!" his father called. "We have to get up, son, even if it is Christmas."

"Aw-right," he said sleepily.

"I'll go on out," his father said. "I'll get things started."

The door closed and he lay still, laughing to himself. The minutes were endless—ten, fifteen, he did not know how many— and he heard his father's footsteps again.

"Rob!"

"Yes, Dad—"

"You son of a—" His father was laughing, a queer sobbing sort of a laugh. "Thought you'd fool me, did you?"

"It's for Christmas, Dad!"

His father sat on the bed and clutched him in a great hug. It was dark and they could not see each other's faces.

"Son, I thank you. Nobody ever did a nicer thing—"

"Oh, Dad." He did not know what to say. His heart was bursting with love.

"Well, I reckon I can go back to bed," his father said after a moment. "No, listen—the little ones are waking up. Come to think of it, son, I've never seen you children when you first saw the Christmas tree. I was always in the barn. Come on!"

He got up and pulled on his clothes again and they went down to the Christmas tree, and soon the sun was creeping up to where the star had been. Oh, what a Christmas, and how his heart had nearly burst again with shyness and pride as his father told his mother and made the younger children listen about how he, Rob, had got up all by himself.

"The best Christmas gift I have ever had, and I'll remember it, son, every year on Christmas morning, so long as I live . . ."

They had both remembered it, and now that his father was dead he remembered it alone: that blessed Christmas dawn when, alone with the cows in the barn, he had made his first gift of true love.

On an impulse, he got up out of bed and put on his slippers and bathrobe and went softly upstairs to the attic and found the box of Christmas-tree decorations. He took them downstairs into the living room. Then he brought in the tree. It was a little one—they had not had a big tree since the children went away—but he set it in the holder and put it in the middle of the long table under the window. Then carefully he began to trim it.

It was done very soon, the time passing as quickly as it had that morning long ago in the barn. He went to his library and fetched the little box that contained his special gift to his wife, a star of diamonds, not large but dainty in design. He tied the gift on the tree and then stood back. It was pretty, very pretty, and she would be surprised.

But he was not satisfied. He wanted to tell her—to tell her how much he loved her. It had been a long time since he had really told her, although he loved her in a very special way, much more than he ever had when they were young.

Ah, that was the true joy of life, the ability to love! He was quite sure that some people were genuinely unable to love anyone. But love was alive in him, alive because long ago it had been born in him when he knew his father loved him. That was it: love alone could waken love.

And he could give the gift again and again. This morning, this blessed Christmas morning, he would give it to his beloved wife. He could write it down in a letter for her to read and keep forever. He went to his desk and began his love letter to his wife: *My dearest love . . .*

Then he put out the light and went tiptoeing up the stairs. The star in the sky was gone, and the first rays of the sun were gleaming in the sky. Such a happy, happy Christmas!

*What Ursula was trying to do suddenly
seemed foolish and impulsive.*

A Gift of the Heart
by Norman Vincent Peale

New York City, where I live, is impressive at any time, but as
Christmas approaches it's overwhelming. Store windows blaze
with lights and color, furs and jewels. Golden angels, 40 feet
tall, hover over Fifth Avenue. Wealth, power, opulence . . . nothing
in the world can match this fabulous display.

Through the gleaming canyons, people hurry to find last-
minute gifts. Money seems to be no problem. If there's a
problem, it's that the recipients so often have everything they
need or want that it's hard to find anything suitable, anything
that will really say, "I love you."

Last December, as Christ's birthday drew near, a stranger was
faced with just that problem. She had come from Switzerland to
live in an American home and perfect her English. In return, she
was willing to act as secretary, mind the grandchildren, do
anything she was asked. She was just a girl in her late teens. Her
name was Ursula.

One of the tasks her employers gave Ursula was keeping track
of Christmas presents as they arrived. There were many, and all
would require acknowledgment. Ursula kept a faithful record,
but with a growing sense of concern. She was grateful to her
American friends; she wanted to show her gratitude by giving
them a Christmas present. But nothing that she could buy with
her small allowance could compare with the gifts she was
recording daily. Besides, even without these gifts, it seemed to
her that her employers already had everything.

At night from her window Ursula could see the snowy expanse
of Central Park and beyond it the jagged skyline of the city. Far
below, taxis hooted and the traffic lights winked red and green. It
was so different from the silent majesty of the Alps that at times
she had to blink back tears of the homesickness she was careful

never to show. It was in the solitude of her little room, a few days before Christmas, that her secret idea came to Ursula.

It was almost as if a voice spoke clearly, inside her head. "It's true," said the voice, "that many people in this city have much more than you do. But surely there are many who have far less. If you will think about this, you may find a solution to what's troubling you."

Ursula thought long and hard. Finally on her day off, which was Christmas Eve, she went to a large department store. She moved slowly along the crowded aisles, selecting and rejecting things in her mind. At last she bought something and had it wrapped in gaily colored paper. She went out into the gray twilight and looked helplessly around. Finally, she went up to a doorman, resplendent in blue and gold. "Excuse, please," she said in her hesitant English, "can you tell me where to find a poor street?"

"A poor street, Miss?" said the puzzled man.

"Yes, a very poor street. The poorest in the city."

The doorman looked doubtful. "Well, you might try Harlem. Or down in the Village. Or the Lower East Side, maybe."

But these names meant nothing to Ursula. She thanked the doorman and walked along, threading her way through the stream of shoppers until she came to a tall policeman. "Please," she said, "can you direct me to a very poor street in . . . in Harlem?"

The policeman looked at her sharply and shook his head. "Harlem's no place for you, Miss." And he blew his whistle and sent the traffic swirling past.

Holding her package carefully, Ursula walked on, head bowed against the sharp wind. If a street looked poorer than the one she was on, she took it. But none seemed like the slums she had heard about. Once she stopped a woman, "Please, where do the very poor people live?" But the woman gave her a stare and hurried on.

Darkness came sifting from the sky. Ursula was cold and discouraged and afraid of becoming lost. She came to an intersection and stood forlornly on the corner. What she was trying to do suddenly seemed foolish, impulsive, absurd. Then, through the traffic's roar, she heard the cheerful tinkle of a bell. On the corner opposite, a Salvation Army man was making his traditional Christmas appeal.

At once Ursula felt better; the Salvation Army was a part of life in Switzerland too. Surely this man could tell her what she wanted to know. She waited for the light, then crossed over to him. "Can you help me? I'm looking for a baby. I have here a little present for the poorest baby I can find." And she held up the package with the green ribbon and the gaily colored paper.

Dressed in gloves and overcoat a size too big for him, he seemed a very ordinary man. But behind his steel-rimmed glasses his eyes were kind. He looked at Ursula and stopped ringing his bell. "What sort of present?" he asked.

"A little dress. For a small, poor baby. Do you know of one?"

"Oh, yes," he said. "Of more than one, I'm afraid."

"Is it far away? I could take a taxi, maybe?"

The Salvation Army man wrinkled his forehead. Finally he said, "It's almost six o'clock. My relief will show up then. If you want to wait, and if you can afford a dollar taxi ride, I'll take you to a family in my own neighborhood who needs just about everything."

"And they have a small baby?"

"A very small baby."

"Then," said Ursula joyfully, "I wait!"

The substitute bell-ringer came. A cruising taxi slowed. In its welcome warmth, Ursula told her new friend about herself, how she came to be in New York, what she was trying to do. He listened in silence, and the taxi driver listened too. When they reached their destination, the driver said, "Take your time, Miss. I'll wait for you."

On the sidewalk, Ursula stared up at the forbidding tenement, dark, decaying, saturated with hopelessness. A gust of wind, iron-cold, stirred the refuse in the street and rattled the ashcans. "They live on the third floor," the Salvation Army man said. "Shall we go up?"

But Ursula shook her head. "They would try to thank me, and this is not from me." She pressed the package into his hand. "Take it up for me, please. Say it's from . . . from someone who has everything."

The taxi bore her swiftly back from dark streets to lighted ones, from misery to abundance. She tried to visualize the Salvation Army man climbing the stairs, the knock, the explanation, the package being opened, the dress on the baby. It was hard to do.

Arriving at the apartment house on Fifth Avenue where she lived, she fumbled in her purse. But the driver flicked the flag up. "No charge, Miss."

"No charge?" echoed Ursula, bewildered.

"Don't worry," the driver said. "I've been paid." He smiled at her and drove away.

Ursula was up early the next day. She set the table with special care. By the time she had finished, the family was awake, and there was all the excitement and laughter of Christmas morning. Soon the living room was a sea of gay discarded wrappings. Ursula thanked everyone for the presents she received. Finally, when there was a lull, she began to explain hesitantly why there seemed to be none from her. She told about going to the department store. She told about the Salvation Army man. She told about the taxi driver. When she finished, there was a long silence. No one seemed to trust himself to speak. "So you see," said Ursula, "I try to do a kindness in your name. And this is my Christmas present you. . . ."

How do I happen to know all this? I know it because ours was the home where Ursula lived. Ours was the Christmas she shared. We were like many Americans, so richly blessed that to this child from across the sea there seemed to be nothing she could add to the material things we already had. And so she offered something of far greater value: a gift of the heart, an act of kindness carried out in our name.

Strange, isn't it? A shy Swiss girl, alone in a great impersonal city. You would think that nothing she could do would affect anyone. And yet, by trying to give away love, she brought the true spirit of Christmas into our lives, the spirit of selfless giving. That was Ursula's secret—and she shared it with us all.

CHRISTMAS BELLS

I heard the bells on Christmas Day,
Their old familiar carols play.
And wild and sweet the words repeat
Of peace on earth, good will to men.

I thought how, as the day had come,
The belfries of a Christendom

Had rolled along th' unbroken song
Of peace on earth, good will to men.

And in despair I bowed my head;
"There is no peace on earth," I said,
"For hate is strong, and mocks the song,
Of peace on earth, good will to men."

Then pealed the bells, more loud and deep:
"God is not dead, nor doth He sleep;
The wrong shall fail, the right prevail,
With peace on earth, good will to men."

Till, ringing, singing, on its way,
The world revolved from night to day
A voice, a chime, a chant sublime,
Of peace on earth, good will to men.

Henry W. Longfellow

Their cold house became
warm with Christmas love.

A West Side Christmas Story
by Pat Sullivan

My husband, Chuck, and my sister, Lee, are partners in a heating company in Chicago. Lee is the buyer, hirer, firer, phone answerer, typist, bookkeeper, office girl and coffee maker. She will bring hot soup and sandwiches to a crew in an icy basement at three o'clock in the morning, but she is Hard-Hearted Hannah when it comes to spending company money.

When she puts an "ND" on an expense-account item, or something she thinks is a luxury, her eyes shoot fire—and Chuck, who is usually a very verbal man, and six feet tall, starts to tiptoe around her desk.

One day about a week before Christmas, all the phones in the office seemed to start ringing at once. There were more broken boilers, burned-out fire pots and stuck stack switches than there had ever been before, and the men were working around the clock. I went into the office to help out on the phones, and it was all I could do just to write down the names and addresses of the people without heat. Worst of all, it seemed that everyone who called either had a new baby, an old grandmother or had just got out of the hospital themselves.

One woman called in tears. She lived in the section of Chicago where the rioting, looting and burning had taken place a few months earlier. She had been phoning for several hours, one heating company after another, trying in vain to get a serviceman to work in a black neighborhood. I took the order and promised that a man would be there within the hour. Then she asked if she could pay a little money each week for the service call, and I looked at Lee and repeated the question. She nodded, "Okay," and when I told the customer, Mrs. Jenkins, not to worry, she said, "God bless you, miss," and hung up.

Lee turned the call over to Chuck, as all of the other men were out. "Bump that other call I gave you; they only have a noisy burner. This is a no-heat. Better get right on it." Chuck left and was gone for several hours.

When he came back, he told Lee, "Forget the billing on that one."

She looked at him. "Since when are we in the charity business?"

Then Chuck told us that Mrs. Jenkins was a widow with seven little children. Her house was clean and bare with very few furnishings. The children were thin and hungry-eyed, wearing worn and much patched clothes. After Chuck had got the heat going, one of the smaller boys had shyly come over to watch him pick up his tools, and Chuck patted him on the head and asked, "What did you tell Santa Claus you wanted for Christmas?"

The child looked him right in the eye and answered, "Ain't no more Santa Claus. Mama say he die, no use to ask him for any toys, 'cause he is dead, and we ain't gonna get none anyways."

Lee never said a word, but brusquely handed Chuck another call and told him to get going. We worked, all three of us, most of the night. The next morning Lee called in to tell us that she hadn't heard her alarm and would be in late. Chuck seemed strangely happy to hear this and asked one of the men to watch the phones for a while, then hustled me into my coat. "Can't spend a dime with that woman looking over my shoulder," he grumbled.

When we pulled up in front of a large toy store, I knew what he was up to. He hummed and whistled while he loaded the shopping cart with dolls, games, trucks and space ships. Then we headed to the candy store for filled stockings, striped red-and-white peppermint canes and marzipan figures of pigs, soldiers and ballerinas. We drove through thick snowflakes, bumper to bumper, all the way to the West Side, unloaded the piles of presents and rang Mrs. Jenkins' doorbell.

In we trotted, behind the whooping children, to find a red-cheeked Lee pinning a Christmas Star of Bethlehem on the top of a fragrant pine tree. Nearby was Mrs. Jenkins, smiling through her tears, as she carefully unpacked a Nativity scene and reverently placed the figures of the holy family in the middle of her dining-room table.

"Well, don't just stand there—get busy!" said Lee, tossing a box of tinsel to my open-mouthed husband. "What took you so long?"

He learned his lesson well.

Long Walk Part of Gift
by Gerald Horton Bath

The African boy listened carefully as the teacher explained why it is that Christians give presents to each other on Christmas day. "The gift is an expression of our joy over the birth of Jesus and our friendship for each other," she said.

When Christmas day came, the boy brought the teacher a sea shell of lustrous beauty. "Where did you ever find such a beautiful shell?" the teacher asked as she gently fingered the gift.

The youth told her that there was only one spot where such extraordinary shells could be found. When he named the place, a certain bay several miles away, the teacher was left speechless.

"Why . . . why, it's gorgeous . . . wonderful, but you shouldn't have gone all that way to get a gift for me."

His eyes brightening, the boy answered, "Long walk part of gift."

They gave the ultimate gift and
received the ultimate blessing.

That Ageless Magic
by Loren Young

One recent Christmas I was visiting my parents who live in a mining community in West Virginia. Times were bad; many of the mines had been shut down. As I walked down to the main part of the town to pick up a few last minute things, I noticed a lame man seated on the cold sidewalk. He had a small tin cup which he held up, hopefully, but few people noticed him—or if they did, they didn't let on.

I could see that one leg was missing. Not an unusual sight in a mining community, but a heartbreaking sight—especially on Christmas Eve.

I started toward him reaching into my pocket. In front of me, a young couple stopped near the lame man. The husband, obviously a miner, and his wife were talking in half whispers.

"Please, please," she was saying. He grimaced, unsure.

"We have our Christmas for us and the kids in these bags," she pleaded. "Let's do it, please." The young husband looked down at his wife. Slowly, a smile came over his face and he agreed.

"But we'll have to walk home 'cause I just saved enough for bus fare."

Reaching into her husband's pocket, she pulled out an old black change purse. Then she walked slowly to the lame man and turned the purse upside down. Coins rattled noisily into the old man's cup. "I'm wishin' you a Merry Christmas," she whispered.

Gratefully, the lame man reached out to shake her hand, then her husband's. There was an exchange of small talk before the couple left.

I watched them walk down the street. As they passed the bus station, the husband made a playful start in that direction.

Laughing, his wife pulled him back. They were broke and would have to walk home. But I could tell by the bounce in their steps that it would not be a long walk. When they lightened their purse, they also lightened their hearts, and the joy that comes from giving had worked its ageless magic once again.

READY FOR CHRISTMAS

"Ready for Christmas," she said with a sigh
As she gave a last touch to the gifts piled high.
Then wearily sat for a moment to read
Till soon, very soon, she was nodding her head.
Then quietly spoke a voice in her dream,
"Ready for Christmas, what do you mean?
Ready for Christmas when only last week
You wouldn't acknowledge your friend on the street?
Ready for Christmas while holding a grudge?
Perhaps you'd better let God be the judge."
She woke with a start and a cry of despair.
"There's so little time and I've still to prepare.
Oh, Father! Forgive me, I see what you mean!
To be ready means more than a house swept clean.
Yes, more than the giving of gifts and a tree.
It's the heart swept clean that He wanted to see,
A heart that is free from bitterness and sin.
So be ready for Christmas—and ready for Him."

Anonymous

> The bridge was out and they would not
> make it home for Christmas Eve.

Unexpected Christmas

by Marguerite Nixon

We were well over half way to our farm in East Texas when the storm broke. Lightning flashed, thunder crashed and a tree fell with a great ripping noise. When the rain poured in such a flood that we could not see the road, my husband drove off on to what seemed to be a bit of clearing deep in the piney woods.

As we waited I sensed we would not get to the farm that night to celebrate Christmas Eve with our family. We were sitting there, miserable and dejected, when I heard a knocking on my window. A man with a lantern stood there beckoning us to follow him. My husband and I splashed after him up the path to his house.

A woman with a lamp in her hand stood in the doorway of an old house; a boy of about 12 and a little girl stood beside her. We went in soaked and dripping, and the family moved aside in order that we might have the warmth of the fire. With the volubility of city people, my husband and I began to talk, explaining our plans. And with the quietness of people who live in the silence of the woods, they listened.

"The bridge on Caney Creek is out. You are welcome to spend the night with us," the man said. And though we told them we thought it was an imposition, especially on Christmas Eve, they insisted. After we had visited a while longer, the man got up and took the Bible from the mantel. "It's our custom to read the story from St. Luke on Christmas Eve," he said, and without another word he began:

And she brought forth her firstborn Son, and wrapped Him in swaddling clothes, and laid Him in a manger. . . .

The children sat up eagerly, their eyes bright in anticipation, while their father read on: *And there were in the same country*

113

shepherds abiding in the field, keeping watch over their flocks by night. I looked at his strong face. He could have been one of them.

When he finished reading and closed the Bible, the little children knelt by their chairs. The mother and father were kneeling, and without any conscious will of my own I found myself joining them. Then I saw my husband, without any embarrassment at all, kneel also.

When we arose, I looked around the room. There were no bright-wrapped packages or cards, only a small, unadorned holly tree on the mantel. Yet the spirit of Christmas was never more real to me.

The little boy broke the silence, "We always feed the cattle at twelve o'clock on Christmas Eve. Come with us."

The barn was warm and fragrant with the smell of hay and dried corn. A cow and a horse greeted us, and there was a goat with a tiny, woolly kid that came up to be petted. This is like the stable where the Baby was born, I thought. Here is the manger, and the gentle animals keep watch.

When we returned to the house there was an air of festivity and the serving of juice and fruitcake. Later, we bedded down on a mattress made of corn shucks. As I turned into a comfortable position, they rustled under me and sent up a faint fragrance exactly like that in the barn. My heart said, "You are sleeping in the stable like the Christ Child did."

As I drifted into a profound sleep, I knew that the light coming through the old pine shutters was the Star shining on that quiet house.

The family all walked down the path to the car with us the next morning. I was so filled with the Spirit of Christmas they had given me that I could find no words. Suddenly I thought of the gifts in the back seat of our car for our family.

I began to hand them out. My husband's gray woolen socks went to the man. The red sweater I had bought for my sister went to the mother. I gave away two boxes of candy, the white mittens and the leather gloves while my husband nodded approval.

And when I was breathless from reaching in and out of the car and the family stood there loaded with the gaiety of Christmas packages, the mother spoke for all of them. "We thank you," she said simply. And then she said, "Wait."

She hurried up the path to the house and came back with a quilt folded across her arms. It was beautifully handmade; the pattern was the Star of Bethlehem. I looked up at the tall beautiful pines because my throat hurt and I could not speak. It was indeed Christmas.

Every Christmas Eve since then, I sleep under that quilt, the Star of Bethlehem, and in memory I visit the stable and smell again the corn shucks, and the meaning of Christmas abides with me once more.

He asked the question, "Who is loneliest
at Christmas?" When he got his answer he
went to work.

He's Straightest When He Stoops
by Thomas J. Fleming

Who are the loneliest people at Christmas time? An asphalt
salesman by the name of Dan Vinson asked himself this question
several years ago. At first he decided that men and women in our
prisons must be the loneliest people during the Christmas season.
But, on thinking deeper, he came to the conclusion that the
children of prisoners must be even lonelier. The result was a
unique project.

Since 1943, Dan Vinson, of Oklahoma City, has sent out
millions of Christmas presents to these kids without accepting a
single cash contribution.

"We haven't done a thing until we give a part of ourselves,"
Vinson says. And that is what he asks—and receives—from
hundreds of people in all walks of life. Working in barns, cellars
and attics, Vinson's volunteers sort and package well over a
million toys each year, which have been donated by businessmen
everywhere.

The children who benefit have never heard of Dan Vinson; he
does not want them to know he exists.

"A kid wants a Christmas present from someone he loves,"
Vinson says. "That's our basic idea."

Each year Vinson visits and corresponds with thousands of
convicts and wardens, who have heard of him by word of mouth
alone. Vinson sends each man a list of twenty-one toys. The
imprisoned father checks the ones he wants, volunteers package
the selections and mail them to the father, who re-addresses the
package to his child. The present, then, is actually from the
child's father.

One of Dan Vinson's favorite sayings is the summary of his
philosophy:

"A man never stands so straight as when he stoops to help a child."

TOYS FOR A KING

What gifts to please a little Boy
Who has the whole world for His toy?
Through Him, with Him, and in Him, live
The lovely playthings I would give—
Black branches traced on afterglow,
Blue moonlight on the wind-glazed snow,
Music, and singing words—but these
Were always His. Upon my knees
I cannot ask a King to take
The stars He watched His Father make.
Here on the clean straw of His Throne,
I lay the only things I own—
A battered will, a raveled mind,
A broken dream I cannot wind.
If I had come to Him before,
And laid them on the stable floor,
Not scratched and finger-marked with sin.
How new and gay they would have been!
Yet strange things catch a Baby's eyes—
There in His Hand my frayed heart lies.

Mary H. Dwyer

Forgotten by those on the outside, Paul
was facing a lonely Christmas.

The Forgotten Prisoner
by Merlin L. Hershberger

Today we celebrated Christ's birthday here in prison and I
believe He was with us.

There are ten men working in the same department with me.
Ten men, whose crimes were as varied and different as the men
themselves. Yet, most of these men are intelligent and understanding.

As Christmas week began, all of us were eagerly looking
forward to the Christmas packages which would be arriving from
home. For they are the symbol of the love of our families, and
our hope for the future. Nothing is more important to a prisoner
than to know that someone still cares.

With the arrival of the first packages, there were more smiles,
perhaps a little more kindness in our hearts; the problems of
prison life were put aside temporarily. This held true for every
prisoner except one; and that one man threatened our entire
Christmas.

Paul is 26 years of age and well liked by all of us. He could
usually be counted upon to cheer up the rest of us when prison
doldrums crept into us. But Paul had not been receiving mail
lately. He offered various excuses for this: his father traveled a
lot, thus making writing hard . . . his brother couldn't write letters
too well . . . his sister had recently married, and everyone knows
how busy a new bride can be . . .

But Paul was certain he would receive a package. They would
remember him—at least on Christmas.

We, who worked with Paul, knew what kind of a person he
was—full of life and with a heart as big as Christmas itself—we
were sure that out there someone would love him enough to
remember.

Monday came and went, as did Tuesday and Wednesday. Only

two days until Christmas. Paul was now the only one in our prison unit without a package.

By three o'clock, Friday afternoon, the effervescence of Christmas was dead in our department. Where before there had been smiling faces, there were now only scowls.

Paul sat at his work desk now, trying to be oblivious to everything. His eyes were as dull as dirty glass. All of us could see despair and hate being manufactured.

We knew how he felt. Hadn't we at times gone through the same discouragement as mail failed to arrive for us when expected?

Then, without plan or scheme or direction, men began sneaking back to their cells. Soon, in a secluded corner of our department, there accumulated a pile of candy, cigarettes and miscellaneous gifts from the Christmas packages of all these men.

A suitable box appeared. Someone produced a Christmas card. It was inscribed simply: "To you Paul, our friend."

We picked up the package and, a little apprehensively, laid it before Paul; none of us quite sure how it would be received.

Surprised, Paul picked up the card and read it. There was an awkward silence. The air seemed to be charged with an undefinable power; you could feel it as surely as an electrical shock. Of this I am certain; in that moment there seemed to be something more in that room than men and furniture.

Slowly Paul raised his head, and his voice choked with emotion: "I can't pretend that this package takes the place of the one I didn't receive, but of one thing I am sure, it's a better package. It's better because this package represents all you could give. It has come from your hearts. It's the most expensive present ever given to me."

Then, aware for the first time of his tears, he brushed them aside and in an almost inaudible voice said: "Thank you."

It was surprising how many of the so-called "hardened criminals," suddenly developed serious head colds.

And so it was that at three-forty-five this afternoon, some of us learned just what Christmas should mean—a lesson so often forgotten—that we can truly keep only that which we give away.

He spent his Christmas on a
special mission of love.

My Unforgettable Christmas
by Richard A. Myers

Christmas can be an adventure for anyone who does not mind a
little walking or meeting a few unpredictable situations. The
adventure I had just before Christmas 1961 made it the most
memorable of my life.

I was at Fort Monmouth, New Jersey—a reservist called back
to duty during the Berlin crisis. An alert just before Christmas
canceled out my plans to spend the holidays with my parents in
Indiana.

Feeling low, I turned on the radio one morning and happened
to catch an announcement: "The General Post Office in New
York City would welcome volunteers who would like to answer
the letters to Santa Claus which have piled up."

Did they mean *in person?*

It wasn't clear to me, but I was intrigued anyway. An
overnight pass got me to New York on Saturday. With permission
from a clerk in the Dead Letter Department of the Postmaster
General's office, I spent a couple of hours sorting and pondering
over letters to Santa which filled two huge hampers.

I selected four letters with New York addresses and debated
whether to buy the toys asked for. It seemed wiser to let events
develop spontaneously. So whistling *Santa Claus is Coming to
Town,* I started out on my adventure.

The first address took me to Harlem and the apartment of
Grace, who had written to Santa Claus on behalf of her four
children. The door was opened by a clean-cut man of 35. I
explained about the letter to Santa Claus.

"You might call me a new kind of Santa's helper," I said.

Grace's husband was cordial, invited me in, and being a
recently discharged serviceman himself, we quickly struck up a
friendship. Grace was away, but he introduced me to the children

and we had a delightful visit. Reluctantly, he accepted a gift for the children.

My second letter was from Kathleen, a request for toys for her and her sister, signed with many kisses for Santa. When I arrived outside her luxurious brownstone house with brass knobs and kick plates on the doors, I almost turned away. But I finally did knock. Kathleen's mother opened the door and after hearing my story called her daughter. "Santa Claus has sent his helper to see you," she explained.

With wide eyes Kathleen sat down beside me while I explained to her about Christmas and assured her she would not be forgotten.

"Your visit has meant a lot to Kathleen," her mother said to me as I left. "We can give her toys but we can't always give her the joy of this kind of experience."

William—age ten—had written from a location in Spanish Harlem. I ended up in a filthy tenement but was unable to find the exact address. Instead, I found myself talking to a tired woman with five children. Impulsively, I handed her enough money to buy presents for all her brood.

The fourth letter was from Lucille, a young mother who wrote that she was separated from her husband, but hoped that Santa would help her with gifts for her two little girls. When I rang the doorbell, a man answered.

Disconcerted, I tried to explain my mission. Lucille then appeared and invited me inside. "My husband and I are together again," she whispered to me happily.

As I told the couple of my experiences that day, we were soon laughing together in a spirit of friendship. "You see," I explained, "I am the one who is grateful. What better way could a lonely serviceman so enjoy a Christmas adventure."

It was true. All day I had traveled about in subways and on buses. My feet were soaked from the snowy streets. There had been no spectacular experiences; several had been awkward. There had been only one case of real need. But for one whole day, I hadn't thought of myself once and had enjoyed myself thoroughly.

When I went to bed that night there was a glow inside me—deep down. I had found Christmas by giving it away.

Section V
Christmas—A Time for Understanding

Christmas is a time for understanding
People and customs throughout the world,
When for all-too-brief a season,
The banner of peace is unfurled.

Albert Schweitzer's Jungle Christmas
by Glenn Kittler

When Christmas comes to Albert Schweitzer's mission at Lambaréné, the Ogowe River runs at floodtide. Heavy rains have fallen in the Belgian Congo for almost a month, and there is at least another month of them ahead. Along the shores of the river, bursts of jungle flowers serve as landmarks, pointing to everyone's goal: the concrete steps which are the landing pier of the Albert Schweitzer Hospital.

All year the hospital is the center of heavy river traffic: the sick arriving, the cured going home to their distant villages. The morning I came to Lambaréné, fleets of the small dugouts clustered around the pier. Nearby, resting against a big rock, was Dr. Schweitzer, watching, waiting.

For more than 40 years Dr. Schweitzer has made his early morning visit to the river, welcoming patients and dispatching them, quickly and gently, to the clinic, surgery, the leper colony. As many as 250 sick arrive at Lambaréné in a single morning, some coming from 500 miles away—a fortnight's journey in Equatorial Africa.

Schweitzer once said, "I have come to Africa to help rectify some of the evils the white man has inflicted upon his black brother."

This he has done through a lifetime of healing bodies and souls. People are aware that there is something special about this place, and it seems most obvious at Christmas.

A Lambaréné Christmas starts many weeks before December 25. Gifts from European and American friends have a long trip, across oceans, slowly up the Ogowe from Port Gentil or perhaps by small plane from Brazzaville; there is no other way to reach the hospital. Once there, gifts must be carefully and constantly guarded against moisture, fungi, ants, even from birds. The gifts that survive these multiple hazards of travel and of the jungle are all the more treasured.

But, understandably, they are not so treasured as the gifts the staff itself exchanges. Some 25 lay missionaries—mostly Europeans and, because of a hospital's needs, mostly women—work with Schweitzer. They receive no pay, only a vitally needed rest trip home every two years, and many refuse even this.

Mrs. Stella Obermann, matronly widow of a Dutch clergyman and mother of another, has been at Lambaréné almost ten years, and she told me, "A strict rule has always been that we must each make our Christmas gifts ourselves, from odds and ends we save all year."

Each staff member gives—and receives—one gift; names are drawn from Dr. Schweitzer's sun helmet weeks earlier. Then the secret preparations start, if it is possible to keep a secret in the jungle. Out of drawers come familiar wrappings and ribbons, familiar because all have seen them before. They have been used for presents put at a table place on birthday or anniversary mornings.

The Lambaréné staff has little time off, even at Christmas, and so on Christmas Eve everyone is still at work far into the evening. Dinner, as usual, is at 7:30, and the staff has just time to wash, fetch their presents, and hurry to the refectory.

The dining hall stands on high ground, overlooking the long and low hospital buildings, workshops, kitchens, and the administration building, at one end of which is the humble room where Dr. Schweitzer works and sleeps. You sense an immediate warmth in the dining hall. Half a dozen small, green-shaded oil lamps line the long table. The linen is snow-bright; the silver sparkles—a neatness especially impressive compared to the jungle disorder outside.

At the far end of the room is a large floral decoration, typically African: palm leaves, brilliant flowers, bright-colored fruit, vines, branches from the rich green jungle shrubs. Small candles, guarded by tin foil, glow throughout the display, and at the top is a tin foil star. As the staff members enter, they put their gifts in front of the decoration, then go to the table.

Dr. Schweitzer says grace; the meal begins. Schweitzer sits at the middle of the table. On his left is Mathilda Kottman, his first assistant, who came to Lambaréné in 1924. On his right is

Mrs. Schweitzer, a small, lovely woman with a quick mind and a self-deprecating wit.

("Have you seen my lovely parrot?" Mrs. Schweitzer asked me. "I thought I had him trained, but he never talks when I want him to." And: "My husband and daughter have the same birthday. Mine is ten days later; I have always been behind everybody else.")

Because his chores keep him constantly moving, it is only at meals that you can study Dr. Schweitzer closely. Now 82, he is slightly stooped, yet he seems much taller than he is. He is well built; his step is heavy and firm; his hands, now gnarled from manual labor, still have their delicacy from the old days when he was the world's leading performer of Bach organ music.

His eyes are astonishingly blue, sometimes deep in thought, hidden by heavy brows, sometimes so bright with humor that you must smile when you look at him. I was with him one afternoon in the leper colony, a half mile from the hospital, where he was supervising a dozen Africans in the construction of a new ward. The work finished for the day, Schweitzer took off his hat, bowed majestically low to the Africans and said, "I thank you, gentlemen." The Africans laughed and returned the bow. I thought:

This is the man who at 21 was already an outstanding Protestant theologian, who since has written some of the most profound of spiritual books, and who was awarded the Nobel Peace Prize. He could have remained in Europe as one of its intellectual and religious leaders, but at 30 he gave up everything, took a degree in medicine, and went off to the hottest, wettest, most diseased part of Africa.

Schweitzer is merriest at Christmas Eve dinner. After the meal and a brief Bible reading, he plays the piano while others sing carols.

And then it's time to open presents, hand-made and heart-made by the devoted friends. Half of a well-known adage or famous quotation is attached to the present by the giver; the recipient must complete the saying before he can have his present. Stumblings, guesses, mistakes—all highlight the evening's merriment. Finally, after a prayer, the staff goes its separate ways—to bed or back to work.

Early Christmas morning finds everyone at his job; there are no holidays in an African hospital. Mid-morning, staff members give presents to their African helpers, and at noon gifts are distributed to the patients. A religious service follows, usually directed by a nurse. From the Catholic mission across the river, a priest comes to say Mass in the leper village.

By early afternoon, the compound is packed with Africans who have come many miles to spend Christmas with Dr. Schweitzer and his staff. He gives them presents sent to him by people from all over the world: clothes, cooking utensils, tools, toys for children, canned food, seeds for the next planting.

At last, when they are all gathered around him sitting on the ground, he reads them the Nativity story, then says:

"This is the story of God's love for us and the love we should have for each other. At one time when people were sick they were left at the roadside to die, but from Christ we learned that we must care for each other, sick or well, rich or poor, black or white. You must learn this and practice it. The doctors and nurses you see at the hospital have learned it and practice it. Christ is why they are here."

By the time refreshments are served and children perform a playlet of the birth of Christ, the day is well into evening and the staff hurries back to its jobs. After dinner, those who are free gather around for more carols, or simply to chat—soon it is late and time for bed.

And then it is morning again, another day, with everyone up at dawn and at his work, caring for the sick and the poor. Thus, for Dr. Albert Schweitzer and his staff, each one a true missionary, every day is rich with opportunities to demonstrate the charity of Christ's birthday. That is why they are there.

> "We finally decided to leave the presents in
> the hope that some needy people would find them."

Undelivered Gifts
by Wayne Montgomery

Have you ever had the experience of *almost not doing* an act of
thoughtfulness or charity—only to discover later that without this
action on your part a very important experience would not have
happened to someone else?

Whenever I am tempted to be lazy or indifferent in this way, I
inevitably think back to that Christmas in Korea, in 1951.

It was late afternoon on December 24. After a cold, miserable
ride by truck in the snow, I was back at our Command Post.
Shedding wet clothing, I relaxed on a cot and dozed off. A
young soldier came in and in my sleep-fogged condition I heard
him say to the clerk, "I wish I could talk to the Sergeant about
this."

"Go ahead," I mumbled, "I'm not asleep."

The soldier then told me about a group of Korean civilians
four miles to the north who had been forced to leave their
burning village. The group included one woman ready to give
birth. His information had come from a Korean boy who said
these people badly needed help.

My first inner reaction was: how could we ever find the
refugees in this snow? Besides, I was dead tired. Yet something
told me we should try.

"Go get Crall, Pringle and Graff," I said to the clerk. When
these soldiers arrived I told them my plan, and they agreed to
accompany me. We gathered together some food and blankets;
then I saw the box of Christmas packages in the corner of the
office. They were presents sent over from charity organizations
in the States. We collected an armful of packages and started out
by jeep.

After driving several miles, the snow became so blinding that we decided to approach the village by foot. After what seemed like hours, we came to an abandoned Mission.

The roof was gone, but the walls were intact. We built a fire in the fireplace, wondering what to do next. Graff opened one of the Christmas packages in which he found some small, artificial Christmas trees and candles. These he placed on the mantel of the fireplace.

I knew it made no sense to go on in this blizzard. We finally decided to leave the food, blankets and presents there in the Mission in the hope that some needy people would find them. Then we groped our way back to the Command Post.

In April, 1952, I was wounded in action and taken to the hospital at Won Ju. One afternoon while basking in the sun, a Korean boy joined me. He was a talkative lad and I only half listened as he rambled on.

Then he began to tell me a story that literally made me jump from my chair. After he finished, I took the boy to our chaplain; he helped me find an elder of the local Korean church who verified the boy's story.

"Yes, it was a true miracle—an act of God," the Korean churchman said. Then he told how on the previous Christmas Eve he was one of a group of Korean civilians who had been wandering about the countryside for days after North Korean soldiers had burned their village. They were nearly starved when they arrived at an old Mission. A pregnant woman in their group was in desperate condition.

"As we approached the Mission, we saw smoke coming from the chimney," the Korean said. "We feared that North Korean soldiers were there, but decided to go in anyway. To our relief, the Mission was empty. But, lo and behold, there were candles on the mantel, along with little trees! There were blankets and boxes of food and presents! It was a miracle!"

The old man's eyes filled with tears as he described how they all got down on their knees and thanked God for their deliverance. They made a bed for the pregnant woman and built a little shelter over her. There was plenty of wood to burn and food to eat and they were comfortable for the first time in weeks. It was Christmas Eve.

"The baby was born on Christmas Day," the man said. He paused. "The situation couldn't have been too different from that other Birth years ago."

On the following morning American soldiers rescued the Koreans, who later became the nucleus of a Christian church in the village where I was recuperating.

You just never know when you have a special role to play in one of God's miracles.

This message from the Loma tribesmen of Liberia
translated by a missionary tells us something
about the true spirit of Christmas.

Christmas Promise

Whoever on the night of the
Celebration of the Birth of Christ
Carries warm water and a sleeping mat
To a weary stranger,
Provides wood from his own fire
For a helpless neighbor,
Takes medicine to one
Sick with malaria,
Gives food to children
Who are thin and hungry,
Provides a torch for a traveler
In the dark forest,
Visits a timid friend
Who would like to know about Christ
Whoever does these things
Will receive gifts of happiness
Greater than that of welcoming a son
Returning after a long absence,
And though he live to be so old
That he must be helped into his hammock,
And though his family and friends all die
So that he stands as a trunk stripped of branches,
Yet life will be sweet for him,
And he will have peace,
As one whose rice harvest is great,
And who hears his neighbors
Praise the exploits of his youth.
So will you receive happiness
If you do these acts of love and service
On the night of the celebration of Christmas,
The Birth of Christ.

One story explaining how the custom began.

Legend of the Christmas Tree

Today the Christmas tree is a center of our festivities. Topped with a star, and glittering with lights and ornaments, it is a part of the beauty and meaning of the Christmas season.

How did the Christmas tree come to play such an important part in the observance of Christmas?

There is a legend that comes down to us from the early days of Christianity in England. One of those helping to spread Christianity among the Druids was a monk named Wilfred (later Saint Wilfred). One day, surrounded by a group of his converts, he struck down a huge oak tree, which, in the Druid religion, was an object of worship.

As it fell to the earth, the oak tree split into four pieces and from its center sprung up a young fir tree. The crowd gazed in amazement.

Wilfred let his axe drop and turned to speak. "This little tree shall be your Holy Tree tonight. It is the wood of peace, for your houses are built of the fir. It is the sign of an endless life, for its leaves are evergreen. See how it points toward the heavens?

"Let this be called the tree of the Christ Child. Gather about it, not in the wilderness, but in your homes. There it will be surrounded with loving gifts and rites of kindness."

And to this day, that is why the fir tree is one of our loveliest symbols of Christmas.

A beautiful legend about giving and receiving.

Just One Small Candle
by Norman Vincent Peale

Queen Marie of Rumania loved to tell a story about a forest village in her country, and the poor people who lived there. Their poverty was most clearly reflected in the ramshackle church which stood near the town center. When visitors came, villagers often said apologetically, "Some day we're going to build a beautiful cathedral like the one on the other side of the forest."

Oh, how they did admire that neighboring church. In fact, on special occasions, they often trekked through the forest to the cathedral—it just seemed God was nearer to them in this majestic setting.

When they made the trip through the dense forest, however, it was necessary to pass by a well which was supposed to be haunted. It was said that if you didn't throw a coin into the well, something would drag you down into it and you would never be seen again.

One cold, dark Christmas Eve, a little boy named Raul passed by on his way to the cathedral, carrying only a small candle to light his path. Back in the village, Raul's widowed mother was dying. He hoped to place his candle on the altar and pray that she might be spared.

As he came near the well, he heard a moan. It was then he realized that he had forgotten to bring a coin. Terrified, Raul started to run. But he tripped on a root and fell by the well's edge. There he heard a child's voice, "Help me out! Give me your light so I can see my way."

"This candle is for my mother," Raul said, trembling. "I must take it to the altar of the big church so that she will get well."

"Can you refuse me on the night of Christ's birth?" the voice

134

pleaded. The boy thought a moment. Then he threw the candle into the well and fell weeping on his knees in the darkness.

Suddenly, the light returned. Looking up, Raul saw a child stepping out of the well holding the little candle in his hand. "Go back home," said the child. "Your mother will live."

Raul ran home and found his mother waiting for him as though she had never been ill. Later that night, they went together to the shabby village church to give thanks. When they entered they were nearly blinded by the light which streamed from the altar. Bathed in such splendor, the old church was every bit as beautiful as the neighboring cathedral.

"Why, Raul," exclaimed his mother, "there is only one candle on the altar. How can one candle make such light?"

Raul was too awed to speak, for as he knelt before the altar he saw that it was his very own candle. The light he had given away had been given back a thousand-fold.

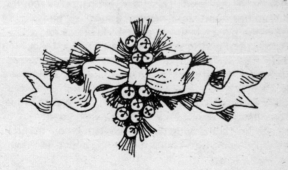

**How one simple act transformed a French
restaurant and unloosed the spirit of Christmas.**

Gift from a Sailor

by Bill Lederer

Admiral David L. McDonald, U.S.N.
Chief of Naval Operations
Washington 25, D.C.
Dear Admiral McDonald:

Eighteen people asked me to write this letter to you.

Last year at Christmas time my wife, our three boys and I
were in France, on our way from Paris to Nice in a rented car.
For five wretched days everything had gone wrong. On Christmas Eve, when we checked into our hotel in Nice, there was no
Christmas spirit in our hearts.

It was raining and cold when we went out to eat. We found a
drab little restaurant shoddily decorated for the holiday. Only
five tables were occupied. There were two German couples, two
French families, and an American sailor by himself. In the
corner a piano player listlessly played Christmas music.

I was too tired and miserable to care. I noticed that the other
customers were eating in stony silence. The only person who
seemed happy was the American sailor. While eating, he was
writing a letter.

My wife ordered our meal in French. The waiter brought us
the wrong thing. I scolded my wife for being stupid.

Then, at the table with the French family on our left, the
father slapped one of his children for some minor infraction, and
the boy began to cry.

On our right, the German wife began berating her husband.

All of us were interrupted by an unpleasant blast of cold air.
Through the front door came an old flower woman. She wore a
dripping, tattered overcoat, and shuffled in on wet, rundown
shoes. She went from one table to the other.

"Flowers, *Monsieur?* Only one *franc*." No one bought any.

136

Wearily she sat down at a table between the sailor and us. To the waiter she said, "A bowl of soup. I haven't sold a flower all afternoon." To the piano player she said hoarsely, "Can you imagine, Joseph, soup on Christmas Eve?"

He pointed to his empty "tipping plate."

The young sailor finished his meal and got up. Putting on his coat, he walked over to the flower woman's table.

"Happy Christmas," he said, smiling and picking out two corsages. "How much are they?"

"Two *francs, Monsieur.*"

Pressing one of the small corsages flat, he put it into the letter he had written, then handed the woman a 20-*franc* note.

"I don't have change, *Monsieur,*" she said. "I'll get some from the waiter."

"No, Ma'am," said the sailor, leaning over and kissing the ancient cheek. "This is my Christmas present to you."

Then he came to our table, holding the other corsage in front of him. "Sir," he said to me, "may I have permission to present these flowers to your beautiful daughter?"

In one quick motion he gave my wife the corsage, wished us a Merry Christmas and departed. Everyone had stopped eating. Everyone had been watching the sailor.

A few seconds later Christmas exploded throughout the restaurant like a bomb.

The old flower woman jumped up, waving the 20-*franc* note, shouted to the piano player, "Joseph, my Christmas present! And you shall have half so you can have a feast too."

The piano player began to belt out *Good King Wenceslaus*.

My wife waved her corsage in time to the music. She appeared 20 years younger. She began to sing, and our three sons joined her, bellowing with enthusiasm.

"*Gut! Gut!*" shouted the Germans. They began singing in German.

The waiter embraced the flower woman. Waving their arms, they sang in French.

The Frenchman who had slapped the boy beat rhythm with his fork against a glass. The lad now on his lap, sang in a youthful soprano.

A few hours earlier 18 persons had been spending a miserable evening. It ended up being the happiest, the very best Christmas Eve they ever had experienced.

This, Admiral McDonald, is what I am writing you about. As the top man in the Navy, you should know about the very special gift that the U.S. Navy gave to my family, to me and to the other people in that French restaurant. Because your young sailor had Christmas spirit in his soul, he released the love and joy that had been smothered within us by anger and disappointment. He gave us Christmas.

Thank you, Sir, and Merry Christmas!

The Christmas Song
by Glenn Kittler

Sadly the young pastor strolled through the snow-covered slopes above the village of Oberndof, Austria. In a few days it would be Christmas Eve, but Josef Mohr knew there would be no music in his church to herald the great event. The new organ had broken down.

Pausing, Pastor Mohr gazed at the scattered lights in the village below. The sight of the peaceful town, huddled warmly in the foothills, stirred his imagination. Surely it was on such a clear and quiet night as this that hosts of angels sang out the glorious news that the Saviour had been born.

The young cleric sighed heavily as he thought, "If only we here in Oberndof could celebrate the birth of Jesus with glorious music like the shepherds heard on that wonderful night!"

Standing there, his mind filled with visions of the first Christmas, Josef Mohr suddenly became aware that disappointment was fading from his heart; in its place surged a great joy. Vividly, he saw the manger, carved from a mountain side; he saw Mary and Joseph and the Child; he saw the strangers who had been attracted by the light of the great star. The image seemed to shape itself into the words of a poem.

The next day he showed the poem to Franz Gruber, the church organist, who said, "These words should be sung at Christmas. But what could we use for accompaniment? This?" Glumly, he held up his guitar.

The pastor replied, "Like Mary and Joseph in the stable, we must be content with what God provides for us."

Franz Gruber studied the poem, then softly strummed the melody that came to him. Next he put the words to the melody and sang them. When he finished, his soul was ablaze with its beauty.

On Christmas Eve, 1818, in a small Austrian village, the Oberndof choir, accompanied only by a guitar, sang for the first time the immortal hymn that begins, "Silent Night . . . Holy Night."

IT WAS THAT NIGHT

It was that ethereal night
when a matchless star stood glowing in the East,
trailing a man, a woman, a burdened beast.

It was that incredible night
when an innkeeper became the first to say:
"I have no room for You this day."

It was that incomparable night
when Gabriel came ecstatic to the earth,
proclaiming glad tidings of a royal birth.

It was that immortal night
when a caring God reached gently down to lay,
His supreme gift, Love, upon the hay.

Fred Bauer

We faced an austere Christmas—prisoners
of the Nazis, but Mother promised a Christmas tree.

Christmas Is a Time for Imagination
by Comtesse De Le Riviere

In 1944 my mother and I were two of the 64 women that
the Nazis held prisoner in a small stable in Ludenburg, Germany.
The other women were Jews and we were the only Christians;
yet, as Christmas approached, Mother and I felt we had to
do something to celebrate the holiday.

"We're going to have a Christmas tree," Mother announced
to me suddenly on Advent Sunday. Then she outlined her plan,
a plan that would have to be carried out in secret.

On Christmas Eve the other women watched with fascination
as we produced a strange collection of treasures and began to
"make" a Christmas tree. First there was a long pole that I
had found in the barn and had kept hidden under my bed.
To this we tied the small pine branches snipped from scraggly
trees once destined for the wood pile. An empty tin can,
laboriously cut apart and shaped, became our "Star of Bethlehem."

For decorations we made bows out of oddments of colored
yarn and festoons cut, kindergarten-style, from scraps of paper.
Often, after air raids, we had found long silvery threads on the
ground. These now served to wrap our tree in gossamer. At last,
after each item had been tied on and in place, we felt that there
was still something missing.

"Candles," Mother said. "If only we had some candles."

And immediately it came to me where I could find some—the
three lanterns in the pig sty. I crept into the Pig's Villa (we called
it that because the accommodations were better than ours) and
sliced off a good, but not too noticeable, chunk from each
candle.

Now our tree came alive. Its light danced in the eyes of all the
women who crowded around it as Mother took out her precious

New Testament and read aloud the message of good cheer. Then, softly we began to sing the old carols, ending with *"Stille Nacht, Heilige Nacht."*

Suddenly the door swung open and in strode Max Wagner, a prison officer.

"What is this?" he demanded roughly.

"It is Christmas Eve," said Mother mildly. "We are celebrating the Holy Evening."

"You Jews?" he asked, incredulously.

"My daughter and I are Christians."

"You're no different. You have Jewish blood."

"So did the first Christians," Mother replied firmly. "Christianity is a matter of faith, not race."

Furious, Wagner grabbed our tree, tore it apart and threw the remains in a corner. Then he stomped out, shutting off the lights.

Later, in the darkness, I stretched out my hand to my Mother's hand searching from the bunk below. "We had our Christmas," she whispered.

That evening, we knew for a certainty that Christmas, no matter how or with what it is celebrated, is eternal. But that particular Christmas was made unforgettable by a tree created out of our imagination.

When Time Stood Still
by Adela Rogers St. Johns

When it comes to God's guidance, which it does every day, every hour, there are many ways we can seek it.

More and more often, more and more surely, with more and more conviction as my need and my faith grow, I have learned to depend on it.

Stand ye still.

Always those words come to me when I ask for guidance, wherever I happen to be, no matter how rushing and noisy it may be inside my mind and out. For to those words I owe the life of my oldest son, Mac.

One December night I awoke sudden and completely, sitting straight up in bed. I was *sure* somebody had called me. When I switched on the light, my clock said 3:15. Getting up, I prowled—a niece, a nephew, one younger son were sleeping in the house. Everyone seemed safe and peaceful.

I do not hear voices, nor see lights, nor catch the echo of bells. But when guidance comes, something irresistible seems to take over. Now the call was distinct in my mind—a call for help.

In the living room, I saw the Christmas tree. Next to the fireplace it stood, slim and green. Tomorrow we'd hang it with bright colors and put the Christmas angel on the top—the one that had been my grandmother's. It was the season of peace on earth, goodwill to men, but there was no peace on earth, this December of 1944. It was the month of the Battle of the Bulge, Bastogne, the Ardennes. My brothers were Marines in the Pacific, my oldest son in France with Patton.

I went back to bed. The call was not from within my home's safe walls. The clock now said 3:25. But it was a different time on islands in the Pacific, on the battlefields of Europe. So I did what, whenever it is possible, is my first step in asking for guidance. I got my Bible from under the detective story with which I'd read myself to sleep, shut my eyes and said, "Father, let me find Your word meant for me. I think one of Your other children needs Your help. I am far away from whoever it is, but You are near us both. Speak to us now through Your word."

In guidance, my experimentation leads me to believe that inner quietness is the first requirement. And the most difficult. Nobody wants to be quiet. Not many of us want to be silent and listen. Prayer is an audience, not an audition; nevertheless, we start telling our Father about the problem and how He ought to solve it.

That's why, when I ask for guidance, to keep my own mind still, I read something: a prayer, a book of inspiration, mostly the Bible. Then I try to be quiet for as long as I am able, in my mind I mean, which is about one minute and 42 seconds; two at the most, as it is with most people. Then I *ask*, with all the expectation and humility that I can generate.

That night I opened the Bible. Just anywhere, where it fell apart.

Stand ye still, and see the salvation of the Lord with you . . . fear not, nor be dismayed, for the Lord will be with you. (II Chronicles 20:17)

Stand ye still. It stood out from the page like copy on a billboard.

And so, simply and directly, I began to pray.

I knew now from whom the call had come, as it had come for many years in many dark nights.

"Father," I prayed, "Your guidance now goes to my son, somewhere in battle, somewhere in danger. Your word goes forth to him and will accomplish what You please for him, which is his safety and his guidance, the light to his feet."

Stand ye still.

I knew, I really did, that this was my guidance and would be my son's. That it had come to me through a channel kept open by prayer and longing and seeking. I went back to sleep in peace.

At breakfast, I told everyone what had taken place. Then it came to me that as it was so near Christmas and everybody always remembers things around Christmas, perhaps Mac would remember something about that early morning hour. So to his APO number I wrote, describing the experience.

His reply reached me soon after Christmas. It said, "Yes I can remember. I was the leader on an I&R (Intelligence and Reconnaissance) platoon; we were out ahead of our regiment, somewhere in the German area, to see if it were safe to move forward. We were moving cautiously, but General Patton was always in a hurry so we were trotting along as fast as we dared.

"All of a sudden it was as though something told me to stop. To stand still. And as I did, out of the corner of my eye, I saw a place on a tree where somebody had chopped off the bark and scrawled in paint the word *Minen*. So I knew it was a mine field. A German soldier had put that sign up to warn his own troops.

"We went back faster than we'd come out, and called up the mine detector squad and, sure enough, there were mines enough to blow up the whole platoon, maybe the Third Army. If I hadn't stopped (and I had to be standing dead-still to see it because it faced the other way) I wouldn't be writing this letter. And we wouldn't have had any Christmas, merry or otherwise."

Maybe you will have another explanation for this!

But to this day it has made a working Christian out of my son Mac. To me it was God's guidance. The voice of His love for us coming through to us.

The first time you receive guidance you will know the difference. You can mistake rhinestones for diamonds, but you can never mistake a diamond for a rhinestone. I know what is true guidance when my mind, my consciousness, whatever we call our mental process, is *thinking* utterly and completely with some thought which I know I have not thought. This comes when the Mind which was in Christ Jesus for which we have prayed takes over.

Prayer for Peace

Lord, make me an instrument of Thy peace.
Where there is hatred, let me sow love;
Where there is injury, pardon;
Where there is doubt, faith;
Where there is despair, hope;
Where there is darkness, light;
Where there is sadness, joy.
O Divine Master, grant that I may not so
　　much seek to be consoled, as to console;
To be understood, as to understand;
To be loved, as to love;
For it is in giving that we receive;
It is in pardoning that we are pardoned;
And it is in dying that we are born to
　　eternal life.

St. Francis of Assisi

The Guideposts Christmas Treasury

SectionVI
Christmas—A Time for Children

Christmas is a time for children
No matter what their age,
Spirit is the only ticket,
And heart the only gauge.

A famous newscaster and his choirboys turn church organ builders. Their deadline was Christmas Eve.

The Christmas Organ
by Leonard E. LeSourd

Dinner was over. Fulton Lewis, Jr. arose from the table and started to his study for a long evening of work on a special broadcast—a task already postponed too many times.

"Tonight," the broadcaster announced with that determined look his family knew so well ... "Tonight I'm not to be disturbed *for anything—not even for St. Peter himself."*

Once in his study, he closed the door firmly and settled himself at his desk. But his mind still rang with the shouts of some thirty harum-scarum youngsters whom, as their choirmaster, he had gathered together that afternoon and conducted on a 60-mile trip to Washington, D.C. for special singing instruction.

Outside he heard the doorbell ring. Rigidly he tried to concentrate on the papers before him, but the sound of youthful voices talking to his wife filtered through.

"Say, we've got something really important to ask Mr. Lewis."

"I'm very sorry, but he just can't be disturbed."

Fulton Lewis sighed, laid down his pen and went out.

"Okay, kids," the broadcaster said dryly, "what's so important?"

Fifteen-year-old Bobby Adams, son of a local bricklayer, spoke up.

"None of us ever heard anything as beautiful as that pipe organ today. We decided to chip in and buy one for our church. How do we go about it?"

"Do you know how much a pipe organ costs?" Lewis asked quizzically.

"As much as $500?"

"About $25,000—for a small one."

The youngsters looked stunned.

"Golly, aren't there any good second-hand ones for less?" wistfully queried 16-year-old Sumpy Readmond, who aspired to be a mechanic. "I'd be glad to help repair it."

Lewis shook his head. "If you want a pipe organ bad enough, you'll have to go out and build one yourselves. Goodnight, kids."

Back at his desk, Lewis squirmed uncomfortably in his chair. "How did I get myself in for all this?"

"All this" referred to the local children and their choir project which music-lover Lewis had taken on months before. It started when many of his neighbors, disturbed by the spiritual drought throughout St. Mary's County, banded together and built a Methodist church outside of the little town of Hollywood, Maryland. Fulton Lewis, Jr., who lived with his family two miles away at Placid Harbor, helped dedicate the sanctuary on his 1947 Christmas Eve broadcast. As a last minute idea, he gathered together a small group of kids for a junior choir.

This new church was a healthy spot in an area peppered with more bars than grocery stores, more gambling joints than churches and many more poor than well-to-do. Youngsters from these families were in the group that approached Fulton Lewis, Jr., several days after the broadcast to ask him to be regular choir-master for their planned junior choir.

Something in their faces grabbed his heart as they came timidly before him with their proposition. His own youngsters, Betsy, 17, and Buddy, 14, had also been working on him. Sure—he'd be glad to train them, but they would have to work harder than ever before.

Who would have imagined that these untrained and often untalented youngsters, ranging from 9 to 17 years, would through persistence, patience and practice, quickly learn some 200 hymns by heart, take to four-part harmony and become a disciplined, imaginative singing body?

But now for his broadcast . . . As he picked up his pen and bent over his papers, the doorbell rang again.

"Mrs. Lewis, could we see Mr. Lewis again for just a minute?"

The broadcaster threw down his pen. "What can you do with a bunch like that?" But there was a twinkle in his eye by the time he reached the front door.

"Mr. Lewis," blurted Bobby Adams, "we decided we can

build a pipe organ. But we need your help—just like with the choir.''

Lewis looked over the youngsters' eager faces and again that same twinge. ''Okay, kids,'' he said, ''you win.'' And fled to his study.

The choir was scheduled for a program at nearby Cedar Point the next evening. At afternoon practice Lewis was jovial. ''You kids tried to put one over on me last night, didn't you? Build a pipe organ! Why, it would take years. What'll you think of next?''

None of their usual banter greeted this. Lewis went on with rehearsal, uncomfortable at their silence.

That night, for the first time, their spark was missing. While driving home, Lewis reflected. All over the country people worried because many youngsters thought only of pleasure and excitement—the kind that led to crime. How often did youth pitch their dreams and hopes in the stars, then have realistic grown-ups dash 'em to the ground?

After the ride home, he gathered them together. ''When we started this choir, I said that if you had faith in yourselves, you could work miracles,'' he began. ''You have with the choir. I tried to discourage you about the pipe organ, but it didn't work. If you'll work twice as hard, we'll tackle the organ.''

Would they!

''Remember this, though . . . No outside professional help. We do the job ourselves—or it doesn't get done. Okay?''

''Okay!''

On the morning of May 17, 1948, villagers along Maryland Highway 235 witnessed an unusual sight. A truck hove into view, piled high with an amazing assortment of pipes. Skeptical townspeople, who well knew that Lewis and several of the choir kids had gone to New York to purchase organ parts, poked a little fun.

''They're stove pipes!''

''Naw . . . 'flub gum' traps,'' cracked another, referring to a certain type of rabbit trap common to local huntsmen.

Lewis pulled up the truck in front of the community church and 700 pipes were quickly disgorged over the church lawn. Kids soon swarmed in from every direction, armed with brushes, buckets of water and glass wax. Overhead the warm rays of a May sun poured down on the scrubbing party as the youngsters bathed and polished pipes, handling delicate parts with a tenderness usually reserved for a precious possession. Local people had never seen anything like it.

Late in the day, grunting, sweating youths reloaded the pipes into a truck for transfer to the Lewis basement. Mrs. Lewis saw at once that her days of orderly housekeeping were over. Her home soon resembled a tool shop as boxes of parts, wires, connections and lumber began to pile up. And pipes everywhere!

Meanwhile, every spare minute, Fulton Lewis pored over a little volume on the technique of organ construction.

Every youngster pitched in. Nothing glamorous about sandpapering the same pipes over and over again . . . or cutting leather diaphragms for the hundreds of needed pneumatics until hands were cramped and aching . . . or twisting wires around contact pins until fingers were raw. The total of 15,000 needed electrical connections seemed staggering.

Mrs. Lewis, resigned to her home becoming a recreational hall, set up her own school—for manners. It wasn't unusual to hear her kind but firm voice lining them up in fives and sixes and instructing them in the art of meeting new people, and introducing each other to strangers. Dedication to their choir and pipe organ projects gave the youngsters a sense of purpose and belonging, something they never had before.

Sumpy Readmond suddenly assumed a mantle of responsibility and leadership. His mechanical ability stood out—for the first time he excelled at something. In his case it was the beginning of a career now under way. Teddy Adams, for another, taught himself to play the organ. Buddy Lewis, the broadcaster's spirited son, was already a skilled organist.

When expenses soared, Choirmaster Lewis became Lecturer Lewis to raise funds. Then, the seemingly insurmountable problem of the "stop list" reared up. The "stop list" is the selection of pipes for various ranks, of which every pipe organ has many, including the flute, trumpet, oboe, chimes, vox humana, reed and diapason. Every rank contains a whole range of pipes, each with a different tone in much the same manner as a piano has a whole range of keys. Keen sensitivity is needed in the selection or the organ tones will be flat.

One day a visitor stood outside the Lewis door.

"Joe Whitefield!" Fulton Lewis cried as he spied his lawyer friend from Washington, D.C., "you're an answer to prayer."

Joe was an ardent and experienced amateur organist. He hardly had his coat off before he was down in the basement, listening to problems involving the "stop list." Snatched up by the fervor of this project, he forgot his mission, his job, everything, for days of continuous work. Together the kids and two grown-ups "voiced" over one thousand pipes, separating them into various ranks, testing them again and again for just the right sound.

Days later Joe Whitefield left, his eyes newly lighted from a labor of love. He went back to Washington, quit his career as lawyer and several weeks later phoned Lewis long distance.

"I never did like being a lawyer," he said. "I just needed to rub against some of the fervor of your kids to set me off on the right track. A man's fool not to work at what he loves." Joe took a job with the Aeolian-Skinner Organ Co. of Boston.

Deadline for completion of the pipe organ was set for Christmas—in time for a Christmas Eve broadcast. Schedules were stepped up, and heads threatened to split over the confused jumble of wires, pipes, magnets, bellows, and connections. In November the process of moving all these from the Lewis basement to the church began.

Then it was discovered that part of the church would have to be redesigned before the organ would fit. Walls were knocked down and choir pews replaced. The organ chest was found to be the wrong size and would have to be rebuilt!

Lewis came home that night convinced he'd have to cancel the special broadcast. It was a grim household with little conversation and edgy nerves. After dinner, as both he and son Buddy often did when upset, Lewis sat down at his small electronic organ. He started to play jerkily, belligerent and bitter. Then the music softened. At the end, the powerful yet simple strains of "The Lord's Prayer" cast a hush over the whole house. It would be hard to imagine a more eloquent prayer for God's help and guidance.

The planned Christmas Eve broadcast was not cancelled. Instead, activity redoubled.

December 23rd was Black Thursday. The organ, though installed, needed endless adjustments. Choir members, drained of energy, beset with doubts, were completely listless. After dismissing them all with an optimism he didn't feel, Lewis worked far into the night and all the next day with the organ tuner.

Hours before the service was to start that December 24th, 1948, the little church by the side of the road began to fill. There was leathery Johnny Green, oysterman and blacksmith; old Doc Greenwell, still country doctor at 88; and some 200 others—all that could jam inside the small church. They came to hear a $35,000 pipe organ built by faith and tenacity—yet, would it play?

Lewis took his place at the organ and nodded to Mervill Dean, local merchant, who was stationed inside the organ loft to manipulate the swell shades that regulated the organ sounds. There hadn't been time to fix the automatic control.

At 7 p.m. the N.Y. radio technician nodded to Lewis. Then the soft strains of *Adeste Fidelis* floated through the church. Garbed in maroon and white gowns, big black collars and white windsor ties, the junior choir marched down the aisle, their exultant voices joining the triumphant organ strains. Lewis, feeling the surging tones of the organ respond to his slightest touch, was lifted by the pride and devotion in the faces of his 30 "choir brats."

They had called these voices immature. If so, then the pipe organ was immature. Yet how could any voice or piece of craftsmanship be immature when created through long hours of work, discouragement, tears and grinding determination? Tonight their singing was reaching out across the country victoriously because this was music with love and heart and soul.

Organ builder skeptics were convinced, and the radio audience will never forget that broadcast. And parents looked upon their youngsters with new respect. That Christmas Eve a little bit of heaven itself crept into the church by the side of a road.

Sit Next to Me, Please
by Robert H. Rockwell

It was dark when we arrived at the home for boys one evening several years ago, but there was enough light to see the eager youngsters crowded on the porch and inside the doorway. Parentless boys, or one-parent boys, they were. With avid interest they watched our approach. But the 40-mile drive had been a tiring one in heavy traffic after a strenuous work day. Frankly I wasn't too happy about the whole thing.

The trips were projects of our local Kiwanis Club. The last time I had been asked to make this trip, I made an excuse, reasoning to myself, "I send them a check each month. It isn't necessary to put in an appearance at the banquets."

However, the time had come when excuses wouldn't do, and it was embarrassing to refuse. I was a board member, and board members were expected to attend.

"Going to join us tomorrow night?" came the inevitable inquiry from a friend.

"Why, yes, Bill. May I pick you up?"

I did. And here we were at the home.

"This always is a big night for the boys," Bill whispered as we walked to the porch. "It's almost embarrassing the way they enjoy our coming."

Two youngsters, age seven or eight, disengaged themselves from the other small fry and attached themselves to us.

"Will you be my company?" a solemn-eyed towhead pleaded uncertainly as he tugged at my coat.

"Sure thing, Fella!"

"My name's Jimmy. Jimmy Thompson. What's yours?"

I told him. Meanwhile the wide-eyed, evaluating gaze was unnerving. Emotions began to stir under the layers of fatigue.

"First time here, isn't it, Mister? Want me to show you around?"

"I'd like that."

He took me on a tour of inspection and importantly pointed out the gymnasium, the library, and his dorm—a narrow room lined with two rows of small iron beds.

"This is my very own wardrobe. See?" Pride was evident in the tone, but the boy seemed to be having some difficulty in breathing. Had we climbed that last flight of stairs too rapidly?

He opened the door of the not-very-wide metal cabinet and I was appalled at the insufficiency of his worldly goods. Guilty thoughts intruded as I mentally compared his inadequate possessions with the large, garment-filled closet and crammed toy chest of my own son.

"There's the dinner bell! We gotta hurry!" Jimmy exclaimed. "But let's not run, 'cause I've got asthma and I don't breathe good when I hurry or get excited."

Then he stopped me for a moment. "Sit next to me at the table, willya, Mister? Please sit next to me!"

Of course I sat beside him. Bill was at the next table elbow-touching his small host. The guestless boys meanwhile turned their wistful glances continually to the tables boasting adult visitors.

By the time dinner was finished Jimmy and I were buddies. He had revealed that he was fatherless, that his mother worked in a supermarket and came each Sunday to take him home for the day, that he "wasn't much good" at athletics but that when he developed a "good breathin' chest" he'd like to become a ball player. Once when he thought I wasn't looking a slender hand lingered on my arm for a moment.

"This boy needs a father!" I anguished. "He's overflowing with love and there's no one to receive it!"

"Will you come again next month, Mister? If you do I'll save a place for you. Right next to me."

The pleading eyes were almost too much for me. I was having trouble with *my* breathing. Me! The smart guy who didn't want to give up an evening of TV to come here! Who thought generosity came through the checkbook. Why, this tyke had given me more in an hour than I could give to the home in a hundred years!

How selfish I was to consider money alone an adequate gift.

Why does it take so long for most of us to learn that the real gift is of one's self?

"Promise you'll come next month?" The request was wheezed.

"Scout's honor," I replied. To myself, I said, "I'll be here, Jimmy. I wouldn't miss being here for anything, because you will be saving me a place. Right next to you."

Money was too scarce for store-bought presents,
but that didn't keep them from giving.

The Christmas We Will Never Forget
by Margery Talcott

When our son Pete was six, it was a depression year and the bare
essentials were all we could afford. We felt we were richer than
most people, though, in things of the mind and imagination and
spirit. That was a comfort of sorts to us, but nothing a six-year-old
could understand.

With Christmas a week off, we told Pete that there could not
be any store-bought presents this year—for any of us.

"But I'll tell you what we can do," said his father with an
inspiration born of heartbreak. "We can make *pictures* of the
presents we'd *like* to give each other."

For the next few days each of us worked secretly, with smirks
and giggles. Somehow we did scrape together enough to buy a
small tree. But we had pitifully few decorations to trim it with.

Yet, on Christmas morning, never was a tree heaped with such
riches! The gifts were only *pictures* of gifts, to be sure, cut out
or drawn and colored and painted, nailed and hammered and
pasted and sewed. But they were presents, luxurious beyond our
dreams:

A slinky black limousine and a red motor boat for Daddy. A
diamond bracelet and a fur coat for me. Pete's presents were the
most expensive toys cut from advertisements.

Our best present to him was a picture of a fabulous camping
tent, complete with Indian designs, painted, of course, by
Daddy, and magnificent pictures of a swimming pool, with funny
remarks by me.

Daddy's best present to me was a water-color he had painted
of our dream house, white with green shutters and forsythia
bushes on the lawn. My best present to Daddy was a sheaf of
verses I had written over the years, verses of devotion and of sad
things and amusing things we had gone through together.

Naturally we didn't expect any "best present" from Pete. But with squeals of delight, he gave us a crayon drawing of flashy colors and the most modernistic technique. But it was unmistakably the picture of three people laughing—a man, a woman, and a little boy. They had their arms around one another and were, in a sense, one person. Under the picture he had printed just one word: US.

For many years we have looked back at that day as the richest, most satisfying Christmas we have ever had.

A CHRISTMAS PRAYER

Oh Lord, this is a season of light,
 of Bethlehem candles burning,
 of menorahs aglow.
Help me to bask in that light.
In that full radiance
 help me to see
My brother
 as he really is:
 Your child, needful of me.
Help me to sustain that recognition
 of him—of Thee—
 as the seasons turn
 and the night sky, once more,
Is aburst with the brilliance of Your birth.

Gordon Neel

Her wish was the same each Christmas.

Please Fix Rosie
by Frieda Marion

When I was a little girl, Santa Claus not only brought new toys, he mended beloved old ones. Every year, early in December, I would write a note to the jolly old saint: "Dear Santa, please fix Rosie!"

Rosie was an old black rag doll, much battered, whose kind, embroidered eyes viewed the uncertainties of my childhood with calm reassurance. I had other dolls, but none was so close to my heart as Rosie. I took care of the other dolls. Ragged though she was, Rosie took care of me. So every December, with a parting pang, I'd place her on the table with my note to Santa pinned to her torn dress, and go to bed lonely but hopeful.

I never knew exactly what happened to Rosie on these pre-Christmas trips. All I knew was that every year she came back, torn dress mended, almost as good as new. As a result, my belief in Santa lasted far longer than it does with most children. I stoutly held to my conviction even when it made me the laughing stock of the second grade. All I knew was that I wasn't going to risk Rosie's life by lack of faith.

The loving hands that did Santa's work are now at rest, but I still have Rosie with her limp, cotton arms and on her sweet embroidered face a relaxed and sleeping look, as if she knows her mission in this world is over and she now dreams those quiet dreams sacred to faithful, retired rag dolls.

And now at Christmas time, when once again the world turns to the ancient story of rebirth, when the exchange of presents among friends expresses our longing for a peaceful world, I find in my heart among all these things a place for the memory of Rosie's annual restoration.

Surely in the renewed blossoming of a little child's favorite doll lies the meaning of the miracle behind the Christmas story, through which we, too, can be reborn . . . the simple miracle of understanding love.

It was the familiar Nativity story the
children were performing until Innkeeper
Wally Purling did some improvising.

Trouble at the Inn
by Dina Donohue

For years now whenever Christmas pageants are talked about in a
certain little town in the Mid-west, someone is sure to mention
the name of Wallace Purling. Wally's performance in one annual
production of the Nativity play has slipped into the realm of
legend. But the old-timers who were in the audience that night
never tire of recalling exactly what happened.

Wally was nine that year and in the second grade, though he
should have been in the fourth. Most people in town knew that
he had difficulty in keeping up. He was big and clumsy, slow in
movement and mind. Still, Wally was well liked by the other
children in his class, all of whom were smaller than he, though
the boys had trouble hiding their irritation when Wally would ask
to play ball with them or any game, for that matter, in which
winning was important.

Most often they'd find a way to keep him out but Wally would
hang around anyway—not sulking, just hoping. He was always a
helpful boy, a willing and smiling one, and the natural protector,
paradoxically, of the underdog. Sometimes if the older boys
chased the younger ones away, it would always be Wally who'd
say, "Can't they stay? They're no bother."

Wally fancied the idea of being a shepherd with a flute in the
Christmas pageant that year, but the play's director, Miss Lumbard,
assigned him to a more important role. After all, she reasoned,
the Innkeeper did not have too many lines, and Wally's size
would make his refusal of lodging to Joseph more forceful.

And so it happened that the usual large, partisan audience
gathered for the town's yearly extravaganza of crooks and
crèches, of beards, crowns, halos and a whole stageful of
squeaky voices. No one on stage or off was more caught up in
the magic of the night than Wallace Purling. They said later that

he stood in the wings and watched the performance with such fascination that from time to time Miss Lumbard had to make sure he didn't wander onstage before his cue.

Then the time came when Joseph appeared, slowly, tenderly guiding Mary to the door of the inn. Joseph knocked hard on the wooden door set into the painted backdrop. Wally the Innkeeper was there, waiting.

"What do you want?" Wally said, swinging the door open with a brusque gesture.

"We seek lodging."

"Seek it elsewhere." Wally looked straight ahead but spoke vigorously. "The inn is filled."

"Sir, we have asked everywhere in vain. We have traveled far and are very weary."

"There is no room in this inn for you." Wally looked properly stern.

"Please, good innkeeper, this is my wife, Mary. She is heavy with child and needs a place to rest. Surely you must have some small corner for her. She is so tired."

Now, for the first time, the Innkeeper relaxed his stiff stance and looked down at Mary. With that, there was a long pause, long enough to make the audience a bit tense with embarrassment.

"No! Begone!" the prompter whispered from the wings.

"No!" Wally repeated automatically. "Begone!"

Joseph sadly placed his arm around Mary and Mary laid her head upon her husband's shoulder and the two of them started to move away. The Innkeeper did not return inside his inn, however. Wally stood there in the doorway, watching the forlorn couple. His mouth was open, his brow creased with concern, his eyes filling unmistakably with tears.

And suddenly this Christmas pageant became different from all others.

"Don't go, Joseph," Wally called out. "Bring Mary back." And Wallace Purling's face grew into a bright smile. "You can have *my* room."

Some people in town thought that the pageant had been ruined. Yet there were others—many, many others—who considered it the most Christmas of all Christmas pageants they had ever seen.

Mother had a good point: "The den is piled
high with gifts we're giving each other, but . . .
what are we going to give Jesus?"

My Most Memorable Christmas
by Catherine Marshall

Why is one Christmas more memorable than another?

It seldom has anything to do with material gifts. In fact, poor circumstances often bring out the creativity in a family.

But I think the most memorable Christmases are tied in somehow with family milestones: reunions, separations, births and, yes, even death. Perhaps that is why Christmas, 1960, stands out so vividly in my memory.

We spent that Christmas at Evergreen Farm in Lincoln, Virginia—the home of my parents. With us were my sister and her husband—Emmy and Harlow Hoskins—and their two girls, Lynn and Winifred. It meant a typical family occasion with our three children, Linda, Chester and Jeffrey, along with Peter John who was then a senior at Yale. Five children can make an old farmhouse ring with the yuletide spirit.

For our Christmas Eve service, Lynn and Linda had prepared an improvised altar before the living room fireplace. Jeffrey and Winifred (the youngest grandchildren) lighted all the candles. Then with all of his family gathered around him, my father read Luke's incomparable account of the first Christmas. There was carol singing, with Chester and Winifred singing a duet, "Hark, the Herald Angels Sing," in their high piping voices. Then my mother, the story-teller of the family, gave us an old favorite, "Why the Chimes Rang." She made us see the ragged little boy creeping up that long cathedral aisle and slipping his gift onto the altar.

Then she said, "You know, I'd like to make a suggestion to the family. The floor underneath the tree in the den is piled high with gifts we're giving to one another. But we're celebrating Christ's birthday—not each other's. This is His time of year. What are we going to give to Jesus?"

The room began to hum with voices, comparing notes. But Mother went on, "Let's think about it for a few moments. Then we'll go around the circle and each of us will tell what gift he will lay on the altar for Christ's birthday."

Chester, age seven, crept close to his father for a whispered consultation. Then he said shyly, "What I'd like to give Jesus this year is not to lose my temper anymore."

Jeffrey, age four, who had been slow in night training, was delightfully specific, "I'll give Him my diapers."

Winifred said softly that she was going to give Jesus good grades in school. Len's was, "To be a better father, which means a gift of more patience."

And so it went . . . on around the group. Peter John's was short but significant. "What I want to give to Christ is a more dedicated life." I was to remember that statement five years later at the moment of his ordination into the Presbyterian ministry when he stood so straight and so tall and answered so resoundingly, "I do so believe. . . . I do so promise. . . ." Yes at Christmastime, 1960, the ministry was probably the last thing he expected to get into.

Then it was my father's turn. "I certainly don't want to inject too solemn a note into this," he said, "but somehow I know that this is the last Christmas I'll be sitting in this room with my family gathered around me like this."

We gasped and protested, but he would not be stopped. "No, I so much want to say this. I've had a most wonderful life. Long, long ago I gave my life to Christ. Though I've tried to serve Him, I've failed Him often. But He has blessed me with great riches—especially my family. I want to say this while you're all here. I may not have another chance. Even after I go on into the next life, I'll still be with you. And, of course, I'll be waiting for each one of you there."

There was love in his brown eyes—and tears in ours. No one said anything for a moment. Time seemed to stand still in the quiet room. Firelight and candlelight played on the children's faces as they looked at their grandfather, trying to grasp what he was saying. The fragrance of balsam and cedar was in the air. The old windowpanes reflected back the red glow of Christmas lights.

Father did leave this world four months later—on May 1st. His passing was like a benediction. It happened one afternoon as he sat quietly in a chair in the little village post office talking to some of his friends. His heart just stopped beating. That Christmas Eve he had known with a strange sureness that the time was close.

Every time I think of Father now, I can see that scene in the living room—like a jewel of a moment set in the ordinary moments that make up our days. For that brief time real values came clearly into focus: Father's gratitude for life; Mother's strong faith; my husband's quiet strength; my son's inner yearning momentarily shining through blurred youthful ambitions; the eager faces of children groping toward understanding and truth; the reality of the love of God as our thoughts focused on Him whose birth we were commemorating.

It was my most memorable Christmas.

The "gift" she gave her newspaper boy
didn't mean much then.

She Kept Her Promise
by John Markas

The experience happened when I was 13 and seemed hardly worth telling anyone at the time. But now, ten years later, it stands above any other Christmas memory I have.

There were 118 customers on my paper route in Morganton, North Carolina. As Christmas drew near I began to nudge my customers into a "remember the paper boy" mood. I bought 118 cheap Christmas cards, signed them "Your friendly paper boy" and several days before Christmas inserted one card in each paper.

The results were quite satisfactory—in fact, almost spectacular. The standard reply was a dollar bill slipped into an envelope marked "paper boy."

Except for Mrs. Luke Woodbury, a widow known for her devoutness. Mrs. Woodbury was standing at the door when I arrived with her Christmas paper.

"I wanted to thank you personally, Johnny, for your card," she said. "It was a kind and thoughtful act to an old lady."

The warmth of her greeting made me feel a little uneasy.

"I haven't much to give you," she said handing me a few coins, "but I want you to know this: I see you every day when you pass the house. Every day I will pray for you, Johnny. I will pray that God will help you and guide you wherever you go, whatever you do."

She put her hand on my shoulder, almost like a caress, and then went back into her house.

A 13-year-old is more inclined to be uncomfortable than moved by such an experience. I certainly didn't think too much about it at the time. Nor did I have any undue interest in religion.

In the years that followed I saw Mrs. Woodbury on a few

occasions. She always smiled at me in a meaningful way. When I went to Duke University I forgot about Mrs. Woodbury until . . .

Until two years ago when the turning point in my life came at a Fellowship of Christian Athletes' conference. A perfunctory Christian until then, I stepped from the darkness of ordinary living into the brightness and joyousness of a new life with Christ at the center.

Soon after this experience I was giving a talk in Chattanooga in which I re-evaluated my life. I spoke about how lucky I was. For the truth of the matter is that I have had to work very hard for my "C" average in college. As for football, during my high school and early college years I had been short of both weight and talent. Yet somehow I was able to find within myself the extra strength or ability I needed to do what had to be done.

After church a lady told me:

"That was not luck, you've obviously had some people praying hard for you all this time."

This was a sudden new thought. My parents, of course. Their faith always had been strong.

And then I remembered Mrs. Woodbury—and her promise to pray for me. How much I owed her!

A few months ago I discovered that Mrs. Woodbury had entered a Home where she could get special care. As a tribute to her—and the unselfish, thoughtful people who pray for others—I tell this story of what I now consider my most memorable Christmas.

The great motion picture producer
recalls an unusual church service.

A Boy's Finest Memory
by Cecil B. DeMille

During this festive Christmas season, churches all over the country will overflow with worshipers. It wasn't always that way . . .

When I was a boy of ten, our community church, in order to stimulate interest among parishioners, decided to hold services every morning at 8 A.M. for a week. Since we couldn't afford a resident minister, one was acquired from the outside. I do not remember his name. But I shall never forget his strong, kindly face and his prominent red beard.

My father, who was very active in the church, sent me off one cold and rainy morning. I walked alone to the small, wooden sanctuary through a murky gloom. Upon arriving, I could see that no one was present but the red-bearded minister and me.

I was the congregation.

Embarrassed, I took a seat, wondering anxiously what he would do. The hour for the service arrived. Surely he would tell me politely to run along home.

With calm and solemn dignity the minister walked into the pulpit. Then he looked down on me and smiled—a smile of great warmth and sincerity. In the congregation sat a solitary child, but he commenced the service as if the church were crowded to the walls.

A ritual opened the services, followed by a reading lesson to which I gave the responses. Then the minister preached a short sermon. He talked earnestly to me—and to God. When it came time for the offering, he placed the collection plate on the altar railing. I walked up and dropped my nickel into the plate.

Then he did a beautiful thing. He came down to the altar to receive my offering. As he did this, he placed his hand on my head. I can still feel the thrill and sensation of his gentle touch. It won my belief and strengthened my faith. The spirit of truth was in the church with us that morning.

None of us can tell at what moment we step into a boy's life and by a demonstration of love and faith turn him in God's direction.

HOPE FOR THE NEW YEAR

Ring out, wild bells, to the wild sky,
The flying cloud, the frosty light:
The year is dying in the night;
Ring out, wild bells, and let him die.
Ring out a slowly dying cause,
And ancient forms of party strife;
Ring in the nobler modes of life,
With sweeter manners, purer laws.
Ring out false pride in place and blood,
The civic slander and the spite;
Ring in the love of truth and right,
Ring in the common love of good.
Ring out old shapes of foul disease;
Ring out the narrowing lust of gold;
Ring out the thousand wars of old,
Ring in the thousand years of peace.
Ring in the valiant man and free,
The larger heart, the kindlier hand;
Ring out the darkness of the land,
Ring in the Christ that is to be.

Alfred Tennyson

The Guideposts Christmas Treasury

Section VII
Christmas—A Time for Learning

Christmas is a time for learning,
A time when new truths unfold,
And not-so-innocent children
Often teach the old.

Gold, Circumstance and Mud
by Rex Knowles

It was the week before Christmas. I was baby-sitting with our four older children while my wife took the baby for his check-up. (Baby-sitting to me means reading the paper while the kids mess up the house.)

Only that day I wasn't reading. I was fuming. On every page of the paper, as I flicked angrily through them, gifts glittered and reindeer pranced, and I was told that there were only six more days in which to rush out and buy what I couldn't afford and nobody needed. What, I asked myself indignantly, did the glitter and the rush have to do with the birth of Christ?

There was a knock on the door of the study where I had barricaded myself. Then Nancy's voice, "Daddy, we have a play to put on. Do you want to see it?"

I didn't. But I had fatherly responsibilities so I followed her into the living room. Right away I knew it was a Christmas play for at the foot of the piano stool was a lighted flashlight wrapped in swaddling clothes lying in a shoe box.

Rex (age 6) came in wearing my bathrobe and carrying a mop handle. He sat on the stool, looked at the flashlight. Nancy (10) draped a sheet over her head, stood behind Rex and began, "I'm Mary and this boy is Joseph. Usually in this play Joseph stands up and Mary sits down. But Mary sitting down is taller than Joseph standing up so we thought it looked better this way."

Enter Trudy (4) at a full run. She never has learned to walk. There were pillowcases over her arms. She spread them wide and said only, "I'm an angel."

Then came Anne (8). I knew right away she represented a wise man. In the first place she moved like she was riding a camel (she had on her mother's high heels). And she was

173

bedecked with all the jewelry available. On a pillow she carried three items, undoubtedly gold, frankincense, and myrrh.

She undulated across the room, bowed to the flashlight, to Mary, to Joseph, to the angel, and to me and then announced, "I am all three wise men. I bring precious gifts: gold, circumstance, and mud."

That was all. The play was over. I didn't laugh. I prayed. How near the truth Anne was! We come at Christmas burdened down with gold—with the showy gift and the tinsely tree. Under the circumstances we can do no other, circumstances of our time and place and custom. And it seems a bit like mud when we think of it.

But I looked at the shining faces of my children, as their audience of one applauded them, and remembered that a Child showed us how these things can be transformed. I remembered that this Child came into a material world and in so doing eternally blessed the material. He accepted the circumstances, imperfect and frustrating, into which He was born, and thereby infused them with the divine. And as for mud—to you and me it may be something to sweep off the rug, but to all children it is something to build with.

Children see so surely through the tinsel and the habit and the earthly, to the love which, in them all, strains for expression.

Too many Santas can be confusing.

A Boy's Christmas Discovery
by Charles E. Lesperance

When my son Larry was six, I drove him through the city showing him dozens of Santas, explaining that they were either volunteers raising funds for the poor or they were on the payrolls of department stores to attract and amuse children.

Then I told him the meaning of Christmas as I understood it. "We celebrate Christmas," I said, "in honor of Jesus, who was born on that day, and we exchange gifts with people we love just as the Three Wise Men brought gifts to the Baby Jesus. Celebrating Christmas is a way of showing that we believe in God and that Jesus was His son. We go to church at Christmas to let God know that we believe."

Larry soberly accepted my explanation. But as Christmas approached, the joy seemed to have gone out of him. Deep down I sensed there had been something missing in my well-meaning attempt to explain that Santa was not the essence of Christmas.

On Christmas Eve our family went to the services at our church; I placed Larry next to me to hold him in case he fell asleep. The service had just begun when I felt him tug at my sleeve. I followed his gaze across the aisle.

There knelt an old man, his cheeks flushed from the cold night, his white beard still aglitter with snowflakes. Protruding from under his heavy overcoat were red pantaloons, tucked into shiny black boots. Dangling from his pocket was a red cap, complete with a big white tassel. His head was bowed, his eyes were closed, his lips moved in prayer.

I was about to lean over and give my explanation to Larry, but before I could speak, Larry looked up, and his expression of enraptured triumph silenced me.

"See, Daddy," he whispered, "Santa Claus believes, too!"

**Christmas is more than a date on the calendar,
it's a state of heart.**

The Gift of a Child
by Mary Ann Matthews

Christmas comes at different times for me every year. I never know precisely when it will arrive or what will produce its spirit, but I can always be sure that it will happen.

Last year Christmas happened while I was visiting my parents in Conneaut, Ohio. The day was frightfully cold, with swirls of snow in the air, and I was looking out of the living room window of my folks' home which faces St. Mary's Church. Workmen had just finished constructing the annual nativity scene in the churchyard when school let out for the day. Children gathered excitedly around the crèche, but they didn't stay long; it was far too cold for lingering.

All the children hurried away—except for a tiny girl of about six. The wind lashed at her bare legs and caused her coat to fly open in the front, but she was oblivious of the weather. All her attention was riveted on the statues before her. Which one I couldn't tell. Was it Mary? The Baby? The animals? I wondered.

And then I saw her remove her blue woolen head scarf. The wind quickly knotted her hair into a wild tangle, but she didn't seem to notice that either. She had only one thought. Lovingly, she wrapped her scarf around the statue of Baby Jesus. After she had covered it, she patted the Baby and then kissed it on the cheek. Satisfied, she skipped on down the street, her hair frosted with tiny diamonds of ice.

Christmas had come once again.

They only had $8 for their father's
Christmas present, that and childlike faith.

Pattern of Love

by Jack Smith, as told to Raymond Knowles

I didn't question Timmy, age nine, or his seven-year-old brother Billy about the brown wrapping paper they passed back and forth between them as we visited each store.

Every year at Christmastime, our Service Club takes the children from poor families in our town on a personally conducted shopping tour. I was assigned Timmy and Billy, whose father was out of work. After giving them the allotted $4 each, we began our trip. At different stores I made suggestions, but always their answer was a solemn shake of the head, no. Finally I asked, "Where would you suggest we look?"

"Could we go to a shoe store, Sir?" answered Timmy. "We'd like a pair of shoes for our Daddy so he can go to work."

In the shoe store the clerk asked what the boys wanted. Out came the brown paper. "We want a pair of work shoes to fit this foot," they said.

Billy explained that it was a pattern of their Daddy's foot. They had drawn it while he was asleep in a chair.

The clerk held the paper against a measuring stick, then walked away. Soon, he came with an open box. "Will these do?" he asked.

Timmy and Billy handled the shoes with great eagerness. "How much do they cost?" asked Billy.

Then Timmy saw the price on the box. "They're $16.95," he said in dismay. "We only have $8."

I looked at the clerk and he cleared his throat. "That's the regular price," he said, "but they're on sale; $3.98, today only."

Then, with shoes happily in hand the boys bought gifts for their mother and two little sisters. Not once did they think of themselves.

The day after Christmas the boys' father stopped me on the street. The new shoes were on his feet, gratitude was in his eyes. "I just thank Jesus for people who care," he said.

"And I thank Jesus for your two sons," I replied. "They taught me more about Christmas in one evening than I had learned in a lifetime."

CHRISTMAS PRAYER FOR YOU

That you may hold forever
    in your heart
        the golden memories
    of every happy Christmas Day
        you have ever known.
That you may be brave in the
    hours of trial when the cross
    is laid upon your shoulders,
when the hill you must climb
        seems very high
and the beacon lights of hope
        are far away.
That every gift God has given you
    may grow with the years
        and fill the hearts
of those you love with its fragrance.
That in every hour
    you may have a friend worthy
        of your friendship
    to whom you can confidently
reach a hand when the storm breaks,
    with whom you can ford the torrent
        and reach the sun-kissed heights.

Patrick F. Scanlan

> "Luis was a special problem at the party.
> He kept trying to take away prizes won by the other boys."

The Winner
by Glenn Kittler

The noise was enough to make Father Bonaventure almost regret having given this party. "The wild Indians are certainly running true to form," he thought.

The children were indeed Indians—members of the Papago tribe, and this was their first Christmas party, given them by the Franciscan priests at the San Xavier Reservation Mission south of Tucson, Arizona.

One boy, Luis Pablo, was a special problem. He kept trying to take away prizes won by other boys.

"Luis!" Father said severely, "why can't you behave?"

"I want to win something," Luis complained.

"Then win something," said Father. "Don't steal it."

At the end of the party the children formed a line and to each Father presented a bag of hard candy. When eight-year-old Luis' turn came he asked, "Can I have three bags?"

"You cannot," said Father sternly. "One bag to each."

"But I mean empty bags."

"Oh! Well, why not?" Father gave Luis three bags and the boy left.

Later, alone in his office, the priest glanced out the window and saw Luis sitting on the school steps. He had three bags open beside him and, carefully, was dividing his candy into them. Then Father Bonaventure suddenly remembered: at home Luis had two brothers and a sister. They were too young to come to the Christmas party. So this was the reason. . . .

The priest went to the party room and scooped the remaining candy into a large bag. It was to go to the Sisters, but he knew that they would not object to what he was about to do. Outside he gave the bag to Luis.

"Here's your prize," he said.

179

"Prize?" Luis asked, suspicious. "What for?"

"All during the party I was watching to see which one of you had the true spirit of Christmas," Father said. "You win."

Then the priest turned and entered the school quickly because he did not want the boy to see his tears.

NOT JUST CHRISTMAS CARDS

One summer my family gave work to a wandering man even though we suspected he had a problem with alcohol. In the fall he left us, but at Christmas a greeting card arrived from hundreds of miles away—no personal message, just a signature. Then, in the spring, he came to see us.

"I've stopped drinking," he said. "I'm going to a permanent job." When we thanked him for his Christmas card, he told us that it was the only card he had sent. "I wanted it to say 'Thank you,' not for the work, but for the respect you gave me. It helped me to begin a new life."

Then there was the lady in the state hospital. She carried the card a friend of ours sent her in a little draw-string bag and during the entire Christmas season she would stop people and say, "Look at my Christmas card. The lady I worked for sent it to me. I'm not forgotten." We heard later that that card, the only one she received, was the beginning of her recovery.

Today I approach Christmas by recalling those two, lone cards. Each represented a new birth at Christmas and both are a reminder to me that Christmas is always a time for remembering.

Reamer Kline

The children taught them all something
about real giving.

The Promise of the Doll
by Ruth C. Ikerman

When I met my friend on the crowded street, she held out her hand to me and said, "I hope you can help me. I'm desperate." Wearily she explained, "I'm about to cry and it's all over a doll. I simply have to find this doll for my granddaughter."

As tears filled her eyes, I remembered the terrible shock we all had felt over the death of her daughter who had been such a vivacious young mother until stricken several months before. The young husband was doing a fine job with the little girl, but it was on the grandmother that much of the burden of planning for good things remained. And this explained her Christmas errand.

"I blame myself entirely," she told me, "for not starting earlier but I never thought it would be a problem to find one of these special dolls. Yet there is not one of this variety left in town."

I asked her, "Well, why can't you settle for another kind of doll?"

She shook her head. "One of the last things my daughter ever said to me before the pain got so bad was how sorry she was that she had refused to buy this doll for her little girl. She told me she had thought the child was too young for such a doll, and had refused to buy it for her birthday, supposing there were lots of occasions ahead when she could get it for her."

Then she told the rest of the story. The little girl had come to her mother's bedside and asked whether the doll might arrive at Christmastime. The young mother grasped the tiny hand in hers and said, "I promise you this for Christmas." Then she had asked her own mother to do this one thing, "Just make sure that my little girl gets that doll this Christmas."

Now my friend was about to fail in her mission. "It's all my fault," she kept repeating. "I waited until too late. It will take a miracle now."

Secretly I agreed, but I tried to keep up a polite facade of courage. "Maybe the child has forgotten, and will be happy with something else."

Grimly my friend replied, "*She* may forget, but I won't." We parted to go our separate ways.

With my mind only half on my shopping, I found the ribbon a neighbor wanted to finish a baby blanket she was making. A few minutes later I stopped at her door to leave the package and was invited inside.

Her two little girls sat on the floor, playing with their dolls. As I sat down, I noticed that one of the dolls was the same type my friend was seeking. Hopefully I asked, "Can you remember where you bought that doll?"

My neighbor gave me her warmhearted smile. "That's not a doll," she said, "she's a member of the family, and as near as I can see she probably was born and not made. She came to us by plane from a favorite aunt in the East."

So I told her that I had a friend who was searching frantically for such a doll for the little girl whose mother had passed away during the year. Apparently unaware of us, the two children played happily. The mother and I spoke in adult words about facing loss at the holiday time, and how much we wished we could help my friend.

Later when I got up to leave, the two little girls followed me to the door.

"Dolly is ready to leave too," they told me. Sure enough, she was dressed in a red velveteen coat and hat with a white fur muff.

"Where is dolly going?" I asked.

They laughed happily. "With you, of course. You know where the lady lives, don't you—the one who needs the doll so bad?"

I started to tell them that of course I couldn't take this doll. Then I looked at their faces, happy in the moment of giving. If I say the wrong thing now, something within my heart warned, I may ruin their joy of giving for the rest of their lives. Silently I took the doll, fumbling with my car keys so they did not see the mist over my eyes.

Their mother asked, "Are you both sure you want to do this?"

They answered, "Yes, we do...." The mother put her arms around them tenderly.

Later I rang the doorbell of my friend. "Don't ask me how I got it, for I can't talk just yet. The doll is a little smudgy, but the worn places are from kisses and maybe they won't show under the Christmas lights."

She fondled the doll as though it were made of precious metal. Tears of joy welled up in the woman's eyes when I finally was able to tell the story.

"How can I ever thank those children enough?" she asked.

"They already have received a blessing greater than anything you or I could give them," I told her. "I saw their faces when they offered me the doll to bring to you."

And it was true. In the moment of giving they had also received, in ways past our finding out. A miracle had taken place. A promise could be kept, linking here with there, in the eternal circle of love of which the great gift of Christmas itself is a part.

He couldn't believe Paul had been
given the new car—free, for nothing.

A Brother Like That
by C. Roy Angell

A friend of mine named Paul received a new automobile from his
brother as a pre-Christmas present. On Christmas Eve, when Paul
came out of his office, a street urchin was walking around the
shiny new car, admiring it. "Is this your car, mister?" he asked.

Paul nodded, "My brother gave it to me for Christmas."

The boy looked astounded. "You mean your brother gave it to
you, and it didn't cost you anything? Free, for nothing? Gosh, I
wish . . ."

He hesitated, and Paul knew what he was going to wish. He
was going to wish he had a brother like that. But what the lad
said jarred Paul all the way down to his heels. "I wish," the boy
went on, "that I could *be* a brother like that."

Paul looked at the boy in astonishment, then impulsively he
added, "Would you like to ride in my automobile?"

"Oh, yes, I'd love that!"

After a short ride the urchin turned, and with his eyes aglow
said, "Mister, would you mind driving in front of my house?"

Paul smiled a little. He thought he knew what the lad wanted.
He wanted to show his neighbors that he could ride home in a
big automobile. But Paul was wrong again.

"Will you stop right where those two steps are?" the boy
asked.

He ran up the steps. Then in a little while Paul heard him
coming back, but he was not coming fast. He was carrying his
little crippled brother. He sat him down on the bottom step, then
sort of squeezed up against him, and pointed to the car.

"There she is, Buddy, just like I told you upstairs. His brother
give it to him for Christmas, and it didn't cost him a cent, and
someday I'm gonna give you one just like it; then you can see

for yourself all the pretty things in the Christmas windows that I've been trying to tell you about.''

Paul got out and lifted the little lad to the front seat of his car. The shining-eyed older brother climbed in beside him and the three of them began a memorable holiday ride.

That Christmas Eve Paul learned what Jesus meant when He said:

It is more blessed to give....

THIS QUIET NIGHT

Hush,
The Baby sleeps
In the arms of His loving mother.
The night is still
And the beasts of the stable hover
Near in soundless adoration.

Hush,
The world's asleep
In the dreams of this loving Infant.
Our hearts are still
And the beasts of our minds take instant
Calm in boundless adoration.

Sleep, Child, sleep
Your sleep of purity.
Sleep, world, sleep
In God's security.

Rehobeth Billings

Why would anyone place a chicken
bone in the collection plate?

The Christmas Wish
by Arthur Gordon

"I don't think it's funny," the Bishop said sharply. He stood up,
and to the young Reverend Thomas Barlow he had never looked
more imposing. "It's in bad taste. It's irreverent. It's—it's
almost sacrilegious!"

Tom Barlow thought wretchedly that it did look odd: the great
silver collection dish, the pile of bills and Christmas offering-
envelopes, and in the middle, naked and unashamed, the wishbone of a large chicken.

"According to the usher," the Bishop said grimly, "this—this
thing came from the Jennisons' pew. Well, the Jennisons may be
as gay in their own home as they like, but this is the house of
God!"

He moved over to the window where eddying snow-flakes
sifted gently. A white Christmas. Until now, a joyous Christmas.
Oh, why, Tom Barlow asked himself, did the Bishop have to
preach his Christmas sermon here?

The Bishop wheeled around. "Barlow, if these people talk
about this indignity, the prestige of the church will suffer. I think
you ought to see them personally and get an apology. This
afternoon."

"This afternoon?"

"This afternoon," said the Bishop. "And take that object with
you!"

The gleaming streets were gay in honor of Christ's birthday,
but driving through them, Tom Barlow felt no answering lift in
his spirits. It was true enough that during his brief pastorate at
Trinity Church he had been trying to attract people like the
Jennisons: young, gay, the "cocktail set" some called them. It
was also true that Cele Jennison looked like a fashion model, and

186

Kirby Jennison had that careless assurance that sometimes made Tom Barlow feel uncomfortable. But sitting in church with their seven-year-old daughter Lisa beside them, they made a handsome sight.

One thing was certain: no apology would be forthcoming from the Jennisons. At best, they would laugh. At worst, they would be angry—and that would end their relationship with Trinity Church.

"Lord," whispered Tom Barlow in one of his sudden, unpremeditated prayers, "You'll have to help me with this. I don't know how to handle it."

The Christmas wreath on the door of the Jennisons' house was enormous; the festive tree in the living room glowed brightly. And yet, it seemed to Tom Barlow, there was an undercurrent of something: tension, friction, unhappiness . . .

"A wishbone in the collection plate?" Cele Jennison burst out laughing. "Oh, how wonderful! I wish I could take the credit, but I can't. As for Kirby—that doesn't sound like him at all!"

Kirby Jennison shook his head. "Not guilty. You don't suppose Lisa . . ."

"Lisa?" Cele Jennison looked startled. "Well, we could ask her . . ."

The child came in, sat down on the long sofa, hands tightly folded. When her mother put the question, she nodded, mutely.

"But why?" said Kirby Jennison. "Why did you do it, Lisa?"

The child said softly, "I wanted God to help me with my Christmas wish."

"What wish?" Tom Barlow said.

The small voice was almost inaudible. "That Daddy and Mummy wouldn't fight. That we'd all be happy, the way we used to be."

Cele Jennison's eyes filled with tears. Kirby Jennison sat very still. It was the Reverend Mr. Barlow who finally moved.

He went to the child, who looked miserable and lost. From his pocket he took the wishbone. "To get your wish, Lisa, you pull it with somebody."

He beckoned to Cele Jennison. She came forward quickly. The snap of the wishbone was loud in the stillness.

"There," said Tom Barlow. "You've got the long end, Lisa.

The long end gets the wish. And just to make *sure* . . ." He held his hand out to Cele Jennison. "Could I have your wedding ring, please?"

She stripped it off with fingers that shook a little. He took it and handed it to her husband. "Now, if you two will just stand together in front of the Christmas tree . . ."

They obeyed him without question.

"Dearly Beloved, we are gathered together here in the sight of God, and in the face of this company . . ."

"Heavens," a faint inner voice voice was saying to Tom Barlow, "the Bishop won't be getting his apology after all." But he found, now, that it didn't matter. These were his people. By remarrying them in the sight of their child, he was helping them to the happiest Christmas of their lives.

At Christmastime, teacher Elizabeth M. Allen of High Point, North Carolina, asked her class of fifth graders to answer this question: "If you could give any gift you wanted to, what would you give and to whom?" Here are some of the responses her students wrote.

One Gift to Give

The gift I would most like to give would be love. It lasts forever and never grows dull. It can be given to anyone that you like.—John Brandon.

If I could give one gift I would give it to my parents. If I could get them to get along together. And live together forever. Year after year, month after month. If I could give that gift, I would give anything in this world if they would live together. And make up their minds if they are going to live together.—Fonda Hunter

I would give a small orphan child friendship, fun and a home where he would be happy. I would tell him never to be sad. —Amanda Greene

I would give jobs and good homes to the poor and stop poverty all over the world.—Laurie Kerr

I would like to give happiness to the people that have not smiled.—Larry Shaw

If I had one gift, I would give it to my mother. I would give her a washer and dryer. Because I love her, and she works too hard.—Darlene Byrd

I would give my crippled grandmother the power to walk. She stays alone down in her home in South Carolina. We left our dog down there to keep her company. She seems real happy when we come; but she gets sad when we leave. She stayed two years in our house, but she wanted to go back home, because she thinks she is too much trouble; but she's not.—Sylvia Johnston

The Guideposts Christmas Treasury

Section VIII
Christmas—A Time for Sharing

Christmas is a time for sharing,
A time for needy hands to clasp,
A time for stretching out in faith
With a reach that exceeds our grasp.

Holiday Candles
by Betty Girling

The most memorable Christmas in my life occurred many years ago when I was eleven. My father and mother had left Ohio to homestead in Nebraska. Our first winter there began bleak and cold and, above all, lonely. We had no neighbors. Once there'd been other homesteaders nearby but they'd moved before we came. Across the fields their cabin stood empty.

In Ohio we'd been used to friends and activity and going to church; but here we lived too far out and my father made the long trip into town only occasionally for supplies.

A few days before Christmas, Pa saddled our horse, Thunder, and rode off to town to get the candles he'd promised for our tree.

Shortly after he left Mother and I were surprised to see a team of horses approaching the empty farmhouse across the field. Soon we could see figures unloading furniture.

"Neighbors!" Mother cried, joyfully.

The next moment she had on her coat and was trudging across our snow crusted cornfields with a loaf of fresh baked bread. Soon Mother was back accompanied by a girl of my age.

"This is Sarah Goodman," she said.

Sarah and I looked at each other shyly. Then I found myself telling her all about the Christmas tree we were going to have when Pa got back from town.

Softly, Sarah said to me: "We're Jewish."

I'd never known a Jewish girl before. Suddenly I felt silly, babbling about trees and candles, and I was sorry for Sarah, not having any Christmas.

"Well, never mind," I told her, struck by a sudden thought, "you have special holidays too, I guess."

"Oh, yes, we have Hanukkah," she began eagerly. "That's

our Feast of Lights . . ." she broke off and jumped to her feet. "Oh, with all the moving, we've forgotten! Why it's already . . ." she counted on her fingers, "it's the fifth day. And I don't even know where we packed the Menorah!" Then with a hasty good-by she ran out and across the fields to her own house.

Mother and I watched her go in surprise, wondering what a "Menorah" might be. Even as we watched it began to snow.

I stayed at the window all afternoon, peering into the white maelstrom. Faster and thicker the snow fell—till I couldn't see Mother's lilac bush a scarce five feet away.

At six Pa had not returned and Mother's face was grim. Here on the plains *blizzard* is a fearsome word. Hadn't they told us in town about the homesteader they found, last winter, frozen to death only four feet from his own barn door?

At 11:00, when Mother finally put me to bed, the blizzard was still raging and Pa had not returned.

At dawn the storm was over. Deep snowdrifts piled high around the house, but the sky was clearing. Mother was sitting in a chair, still waiting. Suddenly we heard shouts and we raced to the door.

Pushing through the drifts came Father, Sarah Goodman and her parents. In they tramped. Soon we were all clustered around the kitchen stove, getting warm.

"It was a miracle," Pa said. "That's what it was, a miracle!"

While mother cooked breakfast Pa told us how he'd got lost in the storm. The road was completely obliterated, he could see nothing in the dark, and had to depend on the horse's instinct for guidance. But finally Thunder wouldn't go on.

"I was nearly frozen by then," Pa said. "So I jumped off the horse and started leading him, just to keep warm. For hours we floundered on. We'd work one way till the drifts got too deep, then turn and work another."

Pa knew he was pretty close to exhaustion when suddenly, through the swirling snow off to one side, he saw some tiny pinpoints of light.

"As I led Thunder toward those lights, I prayed they would still keep shining, and when I reached them I found myself at the Goodmans' cabin. There in the window was a great candlestick, like none I'd ever seen before. Nine candles it held, six of them lighted."

"That was our Menorah," said Sarah, "for Hanukkah, our Feast of Lights. I put it in the window."

"Then you saved Pa's life!"

"Not exactly," said Mr. Goodman, gently. "Sarah really put in on the window sill hoping you would see it and know that she was celebrating her holiday, at this time, like you will be keeping your Christmas."

Mother set us down to breakfast just then and Pa bowed his head, saying: "Almighty God, we thank Thee for the blessings of this season."

When Doctors Served as Theatre Ushers

Christmas was only a few weeks away last year when the Jewish War Veterans of New Brunswick, New Jersey, mobilized volunteers for a unique project. To improve further the already fine community spirit, members offered to replace any Christians who would ordinarily have to work on Christmas Day. The substitutes would accept no pay.

"We placed 60 persons in all," Herman Breitkopf, Jewish Post Commander, reported. "Our volunteers were men and women from all walks of life, including doctors, dentists, nurses, tradesmen, and the like. They acted as theatre ushers, waiters and waitresses and one as an oil truck driver. We had many more standing by to serve as baby sitters, so that Christian families, who otherwise would have had to remain at home, might attend services."

The project advanced the feeling of brotherhood in New Brunswick to a new high, and is a practical plan that almost any community can adapt.

"We plan to continue the program again this year and annually in the future," Mr. Breitkopf stated. "It is our hope that we can serve more and more of our Christian friends each year."

When caring transformed an industrial plant.

The Family in the Parking Lot
by Norman Spray

Have you ever looked at the holidays with a cold and practical eye and then talked yourself into believing that Christmas was not worth all the trouble?

I was making just such a cold and practical appraisal as the Christmas of 1956 approached. On December 11 of that year, another blue-and-purple norther was whistling through our town of Bedford, Texas, and I was in a fittingly icy mood as I drove to work that cold and bleak morning.

I knew that that very morning I faced a deadline on the Christmas issue of the employee news magazine I edited for the Bell Helicopter Company. So far the issue was a mess. Little copy had been written and, worse, my idea well was dry.

"Why should we bother with a Christmas issue anyway?" I asked myself. "In today's busy world who really cares?" Besides, who was I to write a sermon on peace and goodwill to interest men and women who built helicopters? After all, we were publishing a line of communication between management and employees—not a Sunday-school bulletin.

I drove up to the Bell plant. A car was stopped ahead of me, and the driver was talking to the guard at the gate. Beside the driver sat a dark-haired young woman, and in the back, wedged in among a seatful of battered old suitcases, sat a shaggy-haired little boy holding a puppy. The guard pointed directions, and the car drove off toward the visitors parking lot. I didn't know it then, but before the day was out, that car and those people would become important to me.

The driver of that car was Frank Gates, and his wife of four years, Eugenia, sat beside him while their three-year-old son, Frank, Jr., sat in the back. Frank was a logger. He had been

197

working up in Montana, but logging operations had closed down for the winter a week before and Frank had lost his job—again.

He had heard that in Texas he might be able to get year-round work, and so they had loaded their belongings into the old car and headed south. They ate lightly and at night slept in the car because they had barely enough money just for gasoline.

The family had arrived in Fort Worth on the evening of December 10, penniless, bone-tired and famished. Frank had gone to a construction company which happened to be building a new addition to our Bell plant, and they had hired him immediately as a laborer at $1 an hour. That wasn't much, even in those days—unless you'd just arrived from Montana with nothing at all.

"This is it, honey," Frank had said to Eugenia, elated. "From now on, things are going to be better." On that blustery night they had shared a quart of milk and bedded down in the car in high spirits.

"I'm a new man on the construction job out here," Frank had just said to the guard when I first saw him. "Can I park around here?" The guard had no idea that Frank wanted to park his car *and* his family there for the entire day.

At midmorning, the guard captain at plant-security headquarters got a phone call from the gate guard. "A woman and a kid are out here in an old car. They've been here all morning."

The captain and a guard lieutenant went out to speak to the young mother. She looked tired—very tired. "Why," the lieutenant asked, "are you staying in the car?"

Eugenia explained, "We're going to try to find a place when my husband gets off work today."

The two officers both knew that company rules forbade her staying there in the parking lot, so they arranged for Eugenia to park at a service-station lot across the street. While the move was being made they overheard the boy plead, "I'm hungry, Mommy."

Back at the guard office the two security officers told what had happened. It was then that two other guards suggested that they buy lunch for the mother and son. Instantly, $3 was on the table.

One guard carried the money to the plant cafeteria. When the cafeteria manager heard the story, he heaped two plates. "It's on the house," he said.

Eugenia was grateful when the guard handed her the plates,

but when he insisted she take the $3 besides, she became emotional. "Thank you very much," she said, her voice breaking. "But we'll pay you back."

The guard returned to the front-gate guard station. "These are good people, just down on their luck," he told the other guards. "We ought to help them if we can."

The captain and lieutenant went to talk to Frank Gates. "This young fellow's not about to ask anybody for help," the captain said afterward. "All he wants is a chance."

"Trouble is, he won't get paid for two weeks," the lieutenant added.

The last comment left the guards silent. Two weeks is a long time to camp out in a car.

There was a plant rule against employee solicitation, a rule the guards were responsible for enforcing. But in any plant there is a shadowy information network, the grapevine. And at Bell that day, word of the mother's plight swept through the plant. The guards' first act of kindness was multiplied as secretaries and production workers began building a kitty to help a couple they had only heard about.

And that was when I heard about the Gateses, only ten minutes before I was to meet with my boss to talk about the Christmas issue.

Mildly interested, I took a note pad and ambled out to the security office. By then someone had come up with the idea of offering the family some of the clothing that was being collected at the plant for Hungarian relief.

On Frank's lunch hour, the young logger and his family were escorted to the clothes collection point. Hesitantly, they picked a few items: a jacket for Frank, a pair of shoes and overalls for the boy. "This is all we'll need until we get started," said Eugenia. She was careful not to take too much from "those poor people in Hungary."

I went back to my desk and called my wife. I told her about the young Gates family. Barby's reaction was instantaneous—and practical.

"Meet me at their car," she said in the definite tone she reserves for times when she doesn't mean to be questioned. "I'm bringing that woman and her boy home with me."

I walked back to the front gate. A riveter from the factory strode up. "The boys around the plant want this to go to that woman and child out front," he told the guards. "Folks just heard about them and reached for their wallets." He laid $96 on the desk.

Nobody asked any questions—rules or no rules. Another guard, accompanied by the president of the union local, took the gift to Eugenia; I tagged along. There was no fancy speech as the union official said simply, "The folks in the plant want you to have this."

This time, the tired, disheveled Eugenia couldn't hold back the tears. She just sat there, stroking her son's puppy, letting the drops fall unashamedly.

Barby drove up. "I want you to come and visit me until your husband gets off work," Barby said.

Eugenia was hesitant, but she accepted. When Barby brought her back to the plant that afternoon at quitting time, she looked like a new woman, years younger, even radiant. She had napped and bathed and fixed her hair, and Frank, Jr., was sparkling clean. She could hardly wait to rush into the arms of her husband.

"You people are wonderful," he said. "I can't say how wonderful. We'll pay you back. It'll take a little time, but we'll pay you back."

The next morning, Frank appeared on the job 30 minutes before starting time—clean-shaven, rested, the picture of a man with a future. He whistled merrily and strode briskly.

Everyone I met that day wore a cheery smile and had a pleasant greeting. It wasn't imagination—the plant had changed overnight into a friendlier, happier, better place. Suddenly Christmas was everywhere. Suddenly I believed again in its miracle.

In the course of one day I learned that Christmas can never be looked at properly with a cold and practical eye; its value cannot be measured that way. Frank Gates and his family had helped me find a story, and a reason, for the Christmas issue.

Let's Go Neighboring
by Leah Neustadt

This is a country story, about a Christmas away back in 1876.

Uncle Barney was a just and kind man in his ideas of right and wrong. His nearest neighbor was Ed Newton, a good farmer, who had a severe struggle to get along.

Ed Newton watered his milk and was caught at it. You would have to be country bred to know the enormity of the offense. It was on a par with horse stealing, and men have been hanged for that. But we are not all built with stiff backs and incorruptible morals. Ed Newton fell, and was detected. It required money and influence and the pleading and tears of a distracted wife to keep him out of jail. After that he was kept in fierce isolation by his neighbors.

There is no more cruel sentence than to be ignored. When Ed and his family were left alone, Newton became a silent, aged, downcast man who went into the next town to buy his groceries, and have his horses shod. He walked with his head down.

That nearly killed Mary, Ed's wife. She was never again seen at church or at any meetings. You never saw lights in the Newton house at night and Mrs. Newton nursed one of her girls back from the portals of death without even calling the doctor.

The Christmas of 1876 was a stem-winder, with the wind blowing great guns, and the snow drifting until the fences were lost, and the roads almost obliterated. It was bitter cold and the children were sent home from the little red school house. Four inches of ice on the pond had to be chopped through, so the cattle could drink. In the morning came the Christmas calm, the sun shone, and God Almighty showed what a wonderful picture He could make when He set His mind to it.

Simple gifts had been hung in front of the fire-place and there were raisin clusters, stick candy, peanuts, and a great deal of the greatest gift of all, human love in a happy home. The chores had been done, and Uncle Barney sat by the fire toasting his shins, and thinking. His face looked like a graven image, if I know what a graven image is. He kicked off his slippers and reached for his boots.

"Miriam," he said in his rich voice, "you and me and all the children are going visiting. Ed Newton has lived in hell long enough. Even God Almighty don't aim to condemn a man for one slip. Get the dinner fixings together for we are going to eat our Christmas dinner where we ain't invited."

He chuckled and then said, "Maybe I don't look much like a good Samaritan, but I'm going over to try to move a load off a man's heart."

"You are a good and blessed man," came the voice from the kitchen. The children helped to hitch the horse to the big bob-sled with straw in the box and blankets and robes. And the turkey and mince pies were loaded in the clothes basket. Uncle Barney stamped back into the barn and came out with 2 strings of sleigh bells, which he hung on the necks of the snorting horses. Away they all went, down the road, snow flying, crisp air making their cheeks tingle, bells making music, and they swung in the Newton driveway and through a great drift and were at the side door, almost before you could say "Jack Robinson!"

The two women cried out, "Miriam!" and "Mary!" and threw their arms about each other, crying.

Then Uncle Barney said, "We've come neighboring, Ed, just as we used to do, and we want this to be a Merry Christmas for all of us, who need each other and who like each other."

Ed Newton went over to the settee and held his head in his hands, then he got up and kissed his wife and Aunt Miriam and all the girls. And the children got together and played and showed each other's gifts. All the strangeness disappeared.

The women folks then went into the house and started on dinner, while the men folks went out to the barn to look at the stock. The children played in the snow and had a bully time. At last, Mrs. Newton rang the big farm bell on the kitchen roof and they all gathered for Christmas dinner.

Ed Newton said the blessing and choked up so badly that he could hardly get through with it, and his wife laid her worn hand on his while he was praying. Yes, siree, that was some dinner, with two helpings of everything and cider and apples, and nuts in the parlor afterwards.

Well the best of things come to an end. Uncle Barney and his family had to go home for their chores. But visits were promised and all the old troubles were buried deep under the snow, and out of sight. There was more kissing and as Uncle Barney turned back for another handshake, he said, "May God bless this house and all who are in it."

Back in his home, he raked the fire into a blaze and went out and cared for all the animals about the place as becomes a good farmer.

As Uncle Barney started for bed, Aunt Miriam said, "Barney, you are a good man, a blessed good man. God cannot forget what you have done this day."

A Fragile Moment
by E. L. Huffine

The telegram was waiting for me: "Imperative training completed soon as possible. No Christmas leaves authorized."

Then, just before my commanding officer's name, there were the ironic words, "Merry Christmas."

So that was that. There would be no chance to get home, no chance even to try for a little holiday feeling in this fearful year. I was an Army pilot on assignment for special training in celestial navigation at Chicago's Adler Planetarium. This was December, 1941. Our nation had been in World War II for only a few weeks.

Ours was a gloomy bunch that gathered for study in the Planetarium's viewing arena that Christmas Eve. Our teacher realized when she came out to speak that we were not the most receptive of classes.

"Gentlemen," she said, "this is going to be an unusual session. Our engineers have been working since the early hours of this morning in an effort to produce what you are about to see. They want you to accept it as their Christmas gift to you."

Slowly the lights lowered and overhead the stars appeared in view, brighter and brighter, until we were deep in a panorama of dazzling beauty.

"Here are the heavens," the teacher said, her voice soft, her tone reverent. "Here are the heavens just as they were that night when Christ Jesus was born."

Except for a howling wind outside, not a sound could be heard. We stared with the kind of wonder that the shepherds must have known two thousand years earlier. In the midst of war I had a vision of peace and of hope for a sick world that left me breathless.

When the lights came up again, we left the auditorium in

silence. Our gloom was lost as such things are always lost when we let the fact of His birth take over.

THE LOVE THAT LIVES

Every child on earth is holy,
Every crib is a manger lowly,
Every home is a stable dim,
Every kind word is a hymn,
Every star is God's own gem,
And every town is Bethlehem,
For Christ is born and born again,
When His love lives in hearts of men.

W. D. Dorrity

In Another Stable

by David Niven

It took place on Christmas Eve 1939. I had just arrived in
England from Hollywood to volunteer for the British Army.
Having had some previous military experience, I was commissioned
a second lieutenant and given command of a platoon. We were
about to be sent to France and no one was very happy about it.
Most of the men had been conscripted from good civilian jobs;
this was the "phony war" period before the big German attack
of the following spring and it all seemed a big waste of time to
most of them.

Being commanded by a Hollywood actor was an additional
irritant for them and made the whole thing seem even more
ridiculous. The men were not mutinous—but they were certainly
40 of the least well-disposed characters I ever have been associated
with, let alone been in command of.

We were not permitted liberty on that Christmas Eve because
we were due to leave England and our families the next day—a
fine prospect for the holidays. The entire platoon was billeted in
the shabby stables of a farm near Dover.

I could sense the hostility in every soldier. The air was thick
with sarcastic cracks about my bravery in various motion pictures.

It so happens that every night of my life I have knelt down by
my bed and said a simple prayer. But that night I was faced with
a difficult decision. If I suddenly knelt in prayer, here in front of
these men, it occurred to me that 40 tough soldiers would take it
as a final evidence of Hollywood flamboyance.

On the other hand, I have always felt it wrong to avoid saying
my prayers because the situation was not convenient. Besides,
here it was the eve of Christ's birth.

Finally I summoned up my courage and knelt by my bunk. As

I prayed there was some snickering at first, but it soon died away.

When I finished and lay down on the straw, I looked rather sheepishly around the stable and saw at least a dozen soldiers kneeling quietly and praying in their own way.

It was not the first time God had entered a stable—and touched the hearts of men.

It was a special gift, the
first of its kind.

The Erector Set
by Richard H. Schneider

Like many small brothers we were sworn enemies. I'd ride *his* bike, he'd touch *my* train and war was declared.

Christmas was a temporary truce for Herb and me.

Our family celebrated it in Old World fashion—on Christmas Eve. Returning from church services, our parents would usher us through the darkened parlor past the tree, unseen but pungently there, to the kitchen where we'd excitedly wait while dad went out to help Kris Kringle find our house. The doorbell's ring would signal our burst into the parlor. And there Santa would be in full costume—the tree now aglow and the furniture sagging with uncles, aunts and grandparents.

After Santa heard our lies about being "good boys," we'd plunge into our gifts. For Christmas was for *us*—its joy measured by what we *got*.

I was seven the Christmas I'll never forget.

Amid my spoils I came across a clumsily wrapped little package. Unopened in my hand, it already had a strange quality about it. Instinctively I knew it wasn't from my parents.

I turned to my brother; he was watching me.

"It's from me," he said in awe.

Stunned, I slowly opened it.

It was a 25-cent erector set.

Herb had spent all Saturday afternoon picking it out. It represented a half day's work delivering groceries.

His face was aglow with a strange new light of eagerness and concern.

I've long forgotten the other things I got that Christmas Eve. But I'll never forget that little erector set.

For along with it, I'd been given a first vision of God's great gift—that divine joy which floods the heart of the *giver*.

**He didn't live at the North Pole,
but he seemed to be the genuine article.**

Santa Rides the Bus
by Van Varner

Each year, for three weeks only, the old man worked in a department store. Now, December 24th, he pulled himself onto a bus crammed with last-minute shoppers struggling home. The Santa suit was his very own. It was trimmed with white fur as resplendent, almost, as the beard and whiskers that sprang from his smiling face.

A little girl named Doris quickly spotted him. "Look, Danny!" she shouted to her brother, "it's Santa Claus!"

"One of these store-Santas," Danny insisted. Danny was at the age between not really believing, and really wanting to believe.

"He's real, he's real, he's real," Doris chanted.

Danny snorted. "I'll show you how real he is." He bounded from his seat, grabbed the old man's beard and pulled hard.

But the beard did not come off, or even move.

When Danny moved back in embarrassed fright, Santa laughed and lovingly stretched out his hand. Timidly, Danny let Santa lift him onto his knee.

"Do you want to know something, son? You're the first boy to pull my beard all season. And just when I had given up hope!"

Doris also squirmed her way onto Santa's lap. She stared into his face. "Do you live at the North Pole?" she asked.

The old man hesitated. "Hmmmmm," he said. "Now I happen to know exactly where old Santa hangs his coat and hat. If I tell you where, will you promise to remember it always?"

"Oh, yes!"

The whole bus was silent as people leaned forward to hear. "Santa can live anywhere, young lady, but mostly he lives in your heart. He can live in any heart where love lives."

No one spoke for what seemed like a long time. Then the old

man pulled the buzz rope. Gently he kissed Doris on the forehead, and patted Danny. Soon, the doors opened and he stepped out.

Cries of "Merry Christmas, Santa Claus!" followed the old man in the red suit and the great white beard as he disappeared through the door of a big, old house with the sign that read: "Clairville Home for the Aged."

A LASTING CHRISTMAS

I keep a part of Christmas
For it helps to add a glow,
To the January darkness
And the February snow.
If March is cold and blustery
And though April brings us rain,
The peace and warmth of Christmas
With its happiness remain. . . .
There's a beauty when it's Christmas
All the world is different then,
There's no place for petty hatred
In the hearts and minds of men.
That is why my heart is happy
And my mind can hold a dream,
For I keep a part of Christmas
With its peace and joy supreme.

Garnett Ann Schultz

The Christmas spirit is contagious.

Envelope Under the Door
by Hazel Shirley

Two years ago, when I was working in The El Cerrito Variety Store, a freckle-faced boy named Tim Hinch applied for a temporary job to earn some Christmas money. My boss, Harold Pavey, liked his looks and hired him at $10 per week. The job was after school and would last only three weeks.

Our toy department was the busiest section in the store. Lay-away shelves were loaded with packages until Christmas Eve, when only a few remained. One of these packages had been there since early October.

Shortly after lunch, though, the lady who had selected the things in that October package came in to ask if I could help her with a big problem.

She had only two dollars, the lady said, holding back her tears, so that most of the things in her lay-away package would have to go back into stock. Her husband was drinking heavily, and the little she had earned at home doing laundry work was not even enough to feed her four young boys properly. A relative had sent her the two dollars; otherwise there would have been no Christmas gifts at all. I knew she was telling the truth because she lived in my neighborhood and things like that get around.

We had a difficult time trying to make two dollars buy gifts for four boys. Even back in October she had chosen so carefully—jeans, T-shirts, socks, underwear, and one inexpensive toy for each child. She kept picking up a gaily painted ball, then putting it down. Finally she gasped, "I must take this for the baby. He's not even two yet. I want him to have a toy."

I could not say a word. I had a lump as big as a watermelon in my throat.

At last the pathetic little selections were made, and she left with her parcel. Such a small parcel for four small boys!

As soon as she left, Tim, who had heard the conversation, came to me with a ten-dollar bill. "Please give me an envelope and tell me where that lady lives."

"Tim!" I said. "Where did you get that money? You told me this morning you didn't have a dime."

"I asked the boss for my pay ahead of time. He thinks I want to do some last minute shopping."

"Well," I said, "you aren't going to give it to that woman, are you? You need it yourself!"

"I know," Tim replied soberly. "That's why I have to give it to her. My mother had to suffer that same way when we kids were little. You see, I know how it feels. I just have to give it to her." And he kept holding out his hand for the envelope.

I was speechless as I scribbled the name and address for Tim. Then, tucking the bill in the envelope, he looked at me fiercely. "If you ever tell a soul . . ."

I just stood there, watching him go, fighting back the sudden tears. One of the clerks came up and asked what was troubling me.

I took her hand. "Come with me!" I dragged her to the boss's office where I repeated what had happened.

Our boss was—and still is—a wonderful man. He didn't seem to mind our seeing his tears.

Then Christmas really started in that store. The Christmas Spirit, mysterious as always, had made its appearance. And as always, once started, all the gloom or indifference in the world could not stop it. Tim's pay envelope wasn't empty—it was fuller than ever. Everyone tried to do something special for everybody or just anybody.

When Tim returned he was worried. "What if her husband finds the money or one of the kids gets it? I just shoved it under the door . . ."

But in a little while the woman was back, her tired blue eyes shining like stars, so happy and excited she could scarcely talk. "Just imagine," she exclaimed. "There really is a Santa Claus." Showing me the money, she added, "I wish I knew where it came from. Of course I must keep some for food, but I can get some more things from the package, if you still have it."

My boss had already told me what to do. "Don't worry," I told her. "You have more than enough for all the things. Here, the package is all tied up and ready to go."

"But how..."

"Well, you see," I explained hurriedly, "after Christmas we would have to mark the things down so much..." Oh, how I wanted her to believe me!

"Here you are now. You'd better hurry or you'll be late to get your groceries. Merry Christmas!"

A way to make the world a little better.

A Christmas Tradition Continues

Every year at Christmastime Randy Solomon looks just like Santa Claus. As one of the youngest and most unusual of all the season's jolly elves, he carries off the impersonation so well that many youngsters think he's the real Saint Nick. Actually, Randy is a 20-year-old assistant manager of a shoe store in Van Nuys, California, who on each Christmas Eve, for the past three years, unpacks his red Santa suit and begins wrapping gifts—bought with money he has saved during the year.

Then, enlisting his father as a driver, Randy, in long white whiskers and tasseled hat, sets out on his rounds of his community's children's hospitals, plopping his bulging pack beside the bed of an impatient youngster, watching while the child unwraps his gift.

Randy's wholly voluntary mission of joy is a rarity by itself; but what makes it even more unusual is the fact that Randy—who plays such a big part in helping dozens of youngsters celebrate one of the great Christian holidays—is himself Jewish.

The inspiration behind Randy's annual act of charity is his older brother, Don Solomon.

Don had always remembered the days he spent in a hospital when he was six years old. He had left the hospital the day before Christmas, carrying with him the memory of those lonely children he had seen there at holiday time.

In 1960, when he was 18 and had earned money of his own, Don bought a Santa Claus outfit and a pack full of gifts and candy. Then he gained permission to go through the children's wards of hospitals near his home.

After visiting the children's wards, Don made the rounds of his own neighborhood. The kids would flock around him to thank him—or to remind him of the things he had forgotten. Few of the children knew who Santa really was, but they did know that, for them, there *really* was a Santa Claus.

Once as Don came into a hospital ward, a little boy who had been lying listlessly in his bed suddenly jumped up with relief and joy and shouted, "Santa, I've been waiting for you all day long. I knew you'd find me here."

Another time a nurse whispered to Don that a little girl was Jewish and said questioningly, "Perhaps you shouldn't go there?"

Don answered, "That's all right; this Santa is Jewish."

Although Hanukkah, rather than Christmas, is observed in the Solomon home, Don and Randy as kids used to hang up their stockings for Santa to fill with toys and treats.

The Solomons are proud of their Jewish heritage and follow the traditions of their religion. But Don Solomon also followed the tradition of the holiday season that is shared by all faiths—he was a bearer of goodwill to the children he loved, leaving a trail of happiness when he visited and cheered them each Christmas.

Early in December, 1966, just an hour after he had taken his Santa Claus suit out of mothballs to get it ready for Christmas, Don was stricken with a cerebral hemorrhage. He died two days later.

Knowing how much the children meant to Don, Randy stepped in to take his place as Santa Claus. He did it that year as a memorial to Don. But seeing the joyful reaction of the children, Randy has continued to visit the local hospital wards each year since.

It is an act of love for the children and an act of remembrance for Don—and the memory it recalls is a fond one.

"Somehow," his mom says, "we feel the world is a little better today because of Don, and Randy."

An elderly widow receives
an unusual Christmas present.

One Room, One Window
by Eva L. Dunbar

Mrs. Morton was an elderly widow and a permanent tenant in
the guest house where I lived in Oakland, California.

Tony was, to us, simply a sullen man who owned the rooming
house next door.

Once our house had been the mansion of a California senator;
now it was a sheltering stronghold for teachers, business people
and retirees. Many of the dwellings on once-fashionable Jackson
Street, plush landmarks of an earlier era, had become victims of
age. One such was the crumbling white house in which Tony and
his wife lived.

Everyone on the block agreed that Tony was unfriendly, yet
we had to admit that he worked untiringly in his garden and had
restored his weed-rioting premises to prideful order. In that
garden there was a huge magnolia tree, a beautiful tree which
Tony worshipped much as the Druids did their oak. But one
large branch shadowed our house and obscured the view from
the single window of Mrs. Morton's room. Many times the old
lady had wished aloud that the branch were not there. "I do
believe that I could see Lake Merritt," she would say wistfully.
The lake was only a block distant.

Tactfully, Miss Plunkett, our housekeeper, suggested to Tony
that he cut off the branch. He was outraged. Even I, one
courage-giving, brisk October day, hinted to Tony how dark Mrs.
Morton's room was. More outrage.

Then Christmas came. That morning I accompanied Miss
Plunkett on her cheery rounds of the rooms and when we visited
Mrs. Morton, we found her radiantly excited. "Come see!" she
said, tugging us across the room.

Her window now framed a seascape of beauty; diamonds

sparkled on the rippling blue waters of Lake Merritt. The obstructing branch had been cut away.

Miss Plunkett and I hastened next door to thank Tony. I think he was happy to see us, but he shuffled with embarrassment.

"How did you come to do it?" I asked.

Tony groped for expression. "It's Christmas," he said finally.

Christmas, I thought. The old wonderful miracle had repeated itself. Hearts are gentled. Strangers, however self-serving, bring gifts of brotherhood. . . .

"What a lovely gift," Miss Plunkett said.

"But, lady," he said, "*I* got the gift."

We did not know what he meant until, beckoning us outside, Tony pointed, with surprised joy, to his cherished tree. "Look, she's more pretty than before!"

It was true. Removing the wayward limb had destroyed none of the tree's grace. Rather, the magnolia now towered heavenward with sharpened beauty, a symmetry that truly made it the showpiece of Tony's garden, quite the grandest "Christmas tree" on our block.

Section IX
Christmas—A Time for Love

Christmas is a time for love,
A time for inhibitions to shed,
A time for showing that we care,
A time for words too long unsaid.

Their message can change your life.

Three Symbols of Christmas
by Billy Graham

There are three symbols which mean Christmas—the real meaning of Christmas.

The first is a *cradle*. There, in Bethlehem, were cradled the hopes and dreams of a dying world. Those chubby little hands that clasped the straw in His manger crib were soon to open blind eyes, unstop deaf ears and still the troubled seas. That cooing voice was soon to teach men of the Way and to raise the dead. Those tiny feet were to take Him to the sick and needy and were to be pierced on Calvary's cross.

That manger crib in remote Bethlehem became the link that bound a lost world to a loving God.

The *cross*. There were both light and shadow on that first Christmas. There was joy with overtones of sadness, for Jesus was born to die. Jesus, approaching the cross, said, *To this end was I born, and for this cause came I into the world*. To Christians the joy of Christmas is not limited to His birth. It was His death and resurrection that gave meaning to His birth.

It is in the cross that the world can find a solution to its pressing problems.

The *crown*. Jesus was crowned with a crown of thorns and enthroned on a cruel cross, yet His assassins did something, perhaps unwittingly. They placed a superscription over His cross in Greek, Latin and Hebrew: "This is the King."

Yes, Christ is King of kings and Lord of lords, and He is coming back someday. He will come not as a babe in Bethlehem's manger. The next time He comes it will be in a blaze of glory and He will be crowned Lord of all.

Cradle—cross—crown. Let them speak to you. Let the power of Him who came to us at Christmas grip *you*, and He will surely change your life.

A way to keep that spirit
alive—365 days a year.

How to Welcome the Christ Child
by Norman Vincent Peale

Behold, *I bring you good tidings of great joy, which shall be to all people. For unto you is born this day in the city of David a Saviour, which is Christ the Lord.*

No other news ever delivered to human beings can approach in happiness this simple statement of birth. The Scripture says that His name shall be called Emmanuel, which means—God with us. This is the heart of the Christmas message, that Almighty God abides with us.

What a glorious truth! He who rolled back the curtain of the night at the dawn of creation, He who hung the stars in spangled glory upon the skies, He who sets the sun in motion, and the planets according to their orbits, the eternal everlasting Creator and Ruler of the ends of the earth—He, according to this story, is with us; with you and with me. This is the only wonder of the world. The greatest, finest, most intellectual men among us have discovered this truth in their personal experiences.

Why did Christ come? Have you asked yourselves? When last did you think about it?

He came to save the world. To redeem us from our sins. And to show us how to live.

Now those of us who have come to love and serve God, have learned how practical are His teachings, how never failing His help, how ever dependable His advice and directions. We use His way of life, knowing it works daily miracles—and yet we sometimes wonder why it doesn't solve everything.

Is it because we shun the first and real mission of His coming? To save us from our sins—us sinners?

The modern generation does not like to talk about sin; some even go so far as to say there is no sin. Well, what shall we call it? Is it just sophistication? As a matter of fact the word does not

222

apply, because a man who lives a sinful life is not sophisticated, he is a fool. Sophistication means worldly-wise, to know your way around in the world so you will not get licked by the world. But those sinful ones who call themselves sophisticated *are* licked. What is their trouble? They are doing wrong and they cannot stop it. So they try to rationalize it.

Rationalization is when the mind tells you that what you are doing is not wrong—it used to be wrong years ago, but it is not wrong anymore. Whenever you do a wrong thing your mind tries to save face. It always says to you, "Now wait a minute, what you did is not wrong at all; you are really a very fine fellow. These preachers are all out-of-date, behind the times—do not believe them, talking about sin and the like!" That is the way the mind sometimes works.

I once heard a very wise man say something that brought me up short. A university president and author of numerous books, he observed: "The smartest thing the devil ever did was to get people to believe that the devil does not exist."

We believe in God who is a Spirit. We believe in a Universal force that is spiritual. We believe we ourselves have an unperishable spirit. Yes, we believe in the power of the spirit of good. We believe the Bible. But too many of us dismiss the power of the spirit of evil, though we see its work all about us.

The devil, sin? Archaic, childish, old-fashioned, don't you know! And certainly not scientific.

But Christ came to our earth to save mankind from sin—to redeem us—to be our personal salvation. He gave us tools of infinite worth to build our road to Heaven.

Yes, we have a world full of conflict and hate—but God is with us. We cannot save ourselves, but in Him we put our trust.

If today—this minute—we open our hearts and embrace Him and His teachings—not only to reap abundance and joy and health and happy fulfillment, but also for the cancellation of our sins—then this is the greatest welcome we can give to the Christ Child.

What the Star Tells Us
by Fulton J. Sheen

"Why did the Christ Child come?" is a question we often hear at Christmas time. Let us imagine that the star over the crib is five-pointed, and that this light from heaven issued forth five rays which were the reasons for the Christ Child coming to earth.

The first ray was that now God was tabernacled among men. Proud man, who distorted his nature by deifying himself, was given the lesson of Divinity appearing as the servant of men, coming not to be ministered unto, but to minister.

The second ray was His sacrifice. He did not come to live; He came to die. The sin of mankind merited death, for the wages of sin is death. He would take on the sins of man as if they were His own; their blasphemies, as if His lips had spoken them; their thefts, as if His own hands committed them. He became the Good Shepherd Who lays down His life for His sheep.

The third ray was His mercy and compassion and sympathy. He knew human hearts because He made them. Hence His deep love for sinners whom society condemned, and His condemnation of those who sinned and denied they were sinners, or else who sinned but had not yet been found out. Humanity was wounded, but not all men admitted their wounds. But to all who saw their guilt and came to Him, He was the Physician Who restored their souls to union with Himself.

The fourth ray was the establishment of a kingdom which would be a prolongation of His own body. . . . As He taught, as He governed, as He sanctified through other human natures who would be His apostles and their successors, He would continue to teach, to govern and to sanctify.

The fifth ray was His promise to live within us. If He remained on earth, He would have been only an example to be copied; we could have got no closer to Him than an embrace or a word. But if He went back to Heaven and sent His Spirit, then He would be an example to be lived. Those who possess that Spirit of Christ today, manifesting His humility, compassion, sacrifice and love as He did, are really celebrating the Christmas.

Just Another Boy
by Bruce Barton

Sleepless and bewildered but gloriously proud, the husband of Mary emerged from the stable and made his way to the census taker's booth. For it was the decree of Imperial Rome, ordering a general census, that had brought them to Bethlehem.

The angels' song hummed through his heart and timed his steps with its rhythm; his fine, bronzed face was radiant with the wonder of the night. But enrollment blanks and reckonings kept the census taker busy, and all he saw was another peasant standing in the line.

"Name?" he demanded in a routine tone. "Joseph, carpenter, of Nazareth, of the house of David." "Married?" "Yes." "Wife's name?" "Mary." "Children?" The carpenter drew himself up . . . "One Child," he answered proudly. "A son, Jesus, born last night."

Was there any comment? Did the petty government official who wrote for the first time and name that was to be "above every name"—did he wonder as he wrote? Probably not. It was just one more name on the census roll. Just another boy.

What laughter would have rung through Rome if someone had pointed to that name and said: "There is the beginning of the end of your empire and of all empires everywhere." Yet it would have been true. Democracy began, and thrones began to totter when He said: "You are sons of God."

For if all men are sons of God, then all are brothers, and the poorest are entitled to equal rights and privileges with the King.

Rome would have laughed, and Rome is dead. The influence of the Child lives on, uplifting the standards of action and thought, inspiring laws, enlisting the strong in service to the needy and the weak.

We celebrate His birthday, and the festival of all children

226

everywhere. They, not we, are the really important people of the earth. In cradles, and at the foot of Christmas trees, are the lives that are to overthrow and rebuild all that we have built.

Nothing is so powerful or so perfect that it cannot be transformed utterly by the miracle of another girl. Or another boy.

One Solitary Life
by George Clarke Peck

How do you explain the greatness of the Man whose birthday we celebrate on Christmas?

He was born in an obscure village, the child of a peasant woman. He grew up in another village. He worked in a carpenter shop until He was 30, and then for three years was an itinerant preacher. He never wrote a book. He never held office. He never owned a home. He never traveled 200 miles from the place where He was born. He never did one of the things that usually accompany greatness. He had no credentials but Himself.

Although He walked the land over, curing the sick, giving sight to the blind, healing the lame, and raising people from the dead, the top established religious leaders turned against Him. His friends ran away. He was turned over to enemies. He went through the mockery of a trial. He was spat upon, flogged, and ridiculed. He was nailed to a cross between two thieves. While He was dying, the executioners gambled for the only piece of property He had on earth, and that was His robe. When He was dead, He was laid in a borrowed grave through the pity of a friend.

Nineteen wide centuries have come and gone, and today He is the central Figure of the human race and the Leader of the column of progress.

All the armies that ever marched, and all the navies that were ever built, and all the parliaments that ever sat, and all the kings that ever reigned, put together, have not affected the life of man upon this earth as has that One Solitary Life.

By Invitation of Jesus
by Peter Marshall

One bitterly cold December night, when Washington was covered with a blanket of snow and ice, a man sat in his comfortable home on Massachusetts Avenue. A crackling log fire threw dancing shadows on the paneled walls.

The wind outside was moaning softly like someone in pain, and the reading lamp cast a soft, warm glow on the Book this man was reading.

He was alone, for the children had gone out for the evening, and his wife had retired early.

He read the following passage from Luke: . . . *When thou makest a dinner or a supper, call not thy friends, nor they brethren, neither thy kinsmen, nor thy rich neighbors. . . . But when thou makest a feast, call the poor, the maimed, the lame, the blind.*

Somehow he could not get away from those simple words. He closed the Bible, and sat musing, conscious for the first time in his life of the challenge of Christ, whose birthday was so near.

What strange fancy was this? Why was it that he kept hearing in a whisper the words he had just read?

He could not shake it off. Never before had he been so challenged. "I must be sleepy," he thought to himself. "It is time I went to bed."

But as he lay in bed, he thought of the dinners and parties that they had given in this beautiful home. Most of those whom he usually invited were listed in "Who's Who in Washington."

He tried to sleep, but somehow he could not close the door of his mind to the procession of the poor that shuffled and tapped its way down the corridors of his soul.

As he watched them pass, he felt his own heart touched. He whispered a prayer that if the Lord would give him courage, he

229

would take Him at His word, and do what He wanted him to do; only then did he find peace and fall asleep.

When the morning came, his determination gave him new strength and zest for the day.

His first call was on the engraver who knew him well. At the counter he drafted the card, chuckling now and then as he wrote, his eyes shining. It read:

> *Jesus of Nazareth*
> *Requests the honor of your presence*
> *at a banquet honoring*
> *The Sons of Want*
> *on Friday evening, in a home on*
> *Massachusetts Avenue*
> *Cars will await you at the*
> *Central Union Mission*
> *at six o'clock*

At the bottom of the card was the quotation: *Come unto Me, all ye that labour and are heavy laden, and I will give you rest.*

A few days later, with the cards of invitation in his hand, he walked downtown. Within an hour, there were several people wondering what could be the meaning of the card that a kindly, happy, well-dressed man had placed in their hands.

One was an old man seated on a box trying to sell pencils; and another stood on the corner with a racking cough and a bundle of papers under his arms. There was a blind man saying over and over to himself, "Jesus of Nazareth requests the honor of your presence. . . ."

At six o'clock, a strange group of men stood waiting in the vestibule of the Central Union Mission.

"What is the catch in this, anyhow?" asked the cynic. "What's the game?" The blind man ventured to remark: "Maybe it's part of the government relief program."

Just then someone came over and announced that the cars were at the door; without a word, they went outside.

There was something incongruous about it all, these men, clutching their thin coats, huddling together, their faces pinched and wan, climbing into two shiny limousines. At last they were all inside, and the cars glided off with the strangest and most puzzled load of passengers ever carried.

When they dismounted, on Massachusetts Avenue, they stood

gazing at the house. Up the broad steps and over thick-piled carpets, they entered slowly.

Their host was a quiet man, and they liked him—these guests of his, whose names he did not know.

He did not say much, only, "I am so glad you came."

By and by, they were seated at the table, with its spotless linen and gleaming silver. They were silent now; even the cynic had nothing to say. It seemed as if the banquet would be held in frozen silence.

The host rose in his place. "My friends, let us ask the blessing.

"If this is a pleasing to Thee, O Lord, bless us as we sit around this table, and bless the food that we are about to receive. Bless these men. You know who they are, and what they need. And help us to do what You want us to do. Amen."

The blind man was smiling now. He turned to the man seated next to him and asked him about the host. "What does he look like?"

And so the ice was broken; conversation began around the table, and soon the first course was laid.

It was a strange party, rather fantastic in a way, thought the host. His guests had no credentials, no social recommendations, no particular graces—so far as he could see. But, my, they were hungry!

Yet there was not a trace of condescension in his attitude. He was treating them as brothers.

It was a grand feeling—a great adventure.

He watched each plate, and directed the servants with a nod or a glance. He encouraged them to eat; he laughed at their thinly disguised reluctance, until they laughed too.

As he sat there, it suddenly occurred to him how different was the conversation! There were no off-color stories, no whisperings of scandal, no one saying, "Well, I have it on good authority."

They were talking about their friends in misfortune, wishing they were here too . . . wondering whether Charlie had managed to get a bed in the charity ward, whether Dick had stuck it out when he wanted to end it all, whether the little woman with the baby had found a job.

Wasn't the steak delicious!

When the meal was over, someone came in and sat down at

the piano. Familiar melodies, old songs, filled the room; and then in a soft voice the pianist began to sing "Love's Old Sweet Song," "Silver Threads Among the Gold," "The Sidewalks of New York."

Someone else joined in, a cracked wheezing voice, but it started the others. Men who had not sung for months, men who had no reason to sing, joined in.

Before they knew it, they were singing hymns: "What a Friend We Have in Jesus," "The Church in the Wildwood," "When I Survey the Wondrous Cross."

Then the pianist stopped, and the guests grouped themselves in soft, comfortable chairs around the log fire.

The host, moving among them with a smile, said: "I know you men are wondering what all this means; I can tell you very simply but, first, let me read you something."

He read from the Gospels, stories of One who moved among the sick, the outcasts, the despised and the friendless: how Jesus healed this one, cured that one, spoke kindly words of infinite meaning to another, and what He promised to all who believed in Him.

"Now I haven't done much tonight for you, but it has made me very happy to have you here in my home. I hope you have enjoyed it half as much as I have, and if I have given you one evening of happiness, I shall be forever glad to remember it. But this is not my party. It is His! I have merely lent Him this house. He was your *Host*. He is your *Friend*. And He has given me the honor of speaking for Him.

"He is sad when you are. He hurts when you do. He weeps when you weep. He wants to help you—if you will let Him.

"I'm going to give each of you His Book of Instructions. Certain passages in it are marked, which I hope you will find helpful when you are sick and in pain, when you are lonely and discouraged. Then, I shall see each one of you tomorrow, where I saw you today, and we'll have a talk together to see just how I can help you most."

They shuffled out into the night with a new light in their eyes, a smile where there had not been even interest before. The blind man was smiling still, and as he stood on the doorstep, waiting, he turned to where his host stood.

"God bless you, my friend, who-ever you are."

A little wizened fellow who had not spoken all night paused to say, "I'm going to try again, mister; there's somethin' worth livin' for."

The cynic turned back, "Mister, you're the first man who ever gave me anything. And you've given me hope."

"That is because I was doing it for Him," said the host, and he stood and waved good night as the cars purred off into the darkness.

When they had gone, he sat again by the fire and looked at the dying embers, until the feeling became overwhelming, again, that there was Someone in the room. Someone who stood in the shadows and smiled too, because some of the least of these had been treated like brothers for His sake.

Editor's note: Dr. Marshall told this as a story. But many who first heard the sermon felt it must have had basis in fact. We like to think so too.

The Shoemaker's Dream

Once there was a cobbler named Conrad, a godly man. One night Conrad had dreamed that the next day Christ was coming to his humble shop. He got up early the next morning and went to the woods to gather green boughs to decorate his shop so that it would be an appropriate place in which to receive so great a Guest.

He waited all morning, but the only thing happened was that an old man shuffled up, asking to rest. The cobbler saw that his shoes were worn through. "I'll give you a new pair," he said and put on the old man the sturdiest shoes in the shop before sending him on his way.

He waited through the afternoon and the only happening was that an old woman under a heavy load of faggots came by. She was weary, and out of compassion Conrad brought her in and gave her some of the food he had prepared for the Christ Child. Refreshed, she finally went on her way.

Then, as night began to fall, there came into his shop a lost child, crying bitterly. Conrad was annoyed because it was necessary to leave his shop in order to take the child home for she lived on the opposite side of the city.

Returned, he was convinced that he had missed the Lord. Sadly he lived through the moments as he had imagined them: the knock, the call, the latch pulled up, the lighted face, the offered cup. He would have kissed the hands where the nails had been, washed the feet where the spikes had entered. Then the Lord would have sat with him, would have broken bread.

Conrad cried, "Why is it, Lord, that your feet delay? Have You forgotten that this was the day?" Then, soft in the silence a voice he heard:

"Lift up your heart for I kept my word.
Three times I came to your friendly door;
Three times my shadow was on your floor.
I was the beggar with bruised feet;
I was the woman you gave to eat;
I was the child on the homeless street."

They found a way to put
Christ back in Christmas.

The Gift of Double Joy
by Linda Leighton

It happened in 1958. That fall, when my husband, Joe, and I were making out our Christmas shopping list, we suddenly realized that our giving had become almost routine. We wanted to remember our friends at Christmas but we had little enthusiasm for the usual exchange of ties and trinkets.

Then at our church (St. James Presbyterian) we heard a Korean missionary tell of the thousands of destitute refugee children. An idea was born. All our presents would go to these children.

Here, we felt, was a way to really "put Christ back into Christmas."

A missionary in Korea provided us with names, ages, sex and measurements of 35 children. We sent gifts, each bearing the name of one of our friends as the giver. A greeting card from us to our friends announced the gift and the address of the child to whom it had gone.

Many of our friends began correspondence with these youngsters. The idea has spread to others in our church and outside as well.

Every Christmas is now an exciting experience as we find new names of children and new givers. It is surprising—or is it—that this kind of double giving doubles the joy.

The Guideposts Christmas Treasury

Section X
Christmas—A Time for Remembering

Christmas is a time to remember
Timeless stories from days of yore,
A time to ponder what's ahead,
A time to open another door.

Could Frank Sanders withstand the
annual temptation that came every Christmas Eve?

Somebody in the Corner
by John Sutherland Bonnell

Every Christmas Eve, the women of Renshaw, in Nova Scotia, gather at nightfall on the railroad platform. Their children in bed, they come to wait for fathers and husbands, who, having shopped all afternoon in the county seat, are bringing home the Christmas playthings.

When I was a very young man I knew a woman named Emily Sanders who, year after year on Christmas Eve waited there in the frosty starlight, all in vain. This is the story of the man she was waiting for. And while I have changed names and altered facts, here a little and there a little, this is substantially a true account of what befell us there long ago.

It began on a June day, when I was a divinity student filling a summer "practice pulpit" in that orchard land of Evangeline. Bumping along a back-hill road on my secondhand bicycle, I was caught in a sudden and furious thunder storm. Ahead of me, through the downpour, I could see a barefoot little girl sloshing across a rickety wooden bridge.

"Stop crying!" I called to the red-haired moppet; "the bridge is wet enough already."

From behind the seat, I unlashed a collapsible umbrella, and then, with the child straddling in front, and the umbrella held shakily over us, I tried to guide the bike with one hand, on down the hill.

"Where do you live?" I shouted into her ear.

"Second house just at the bottom."

"What's your name?"

"Mary. My father is Frank Sanders. Does that mean I have to get off?"

There was no time to pursue the strangeness of her question; we had arrived. Standing in the doorway was a tall, gaunt woman and the only well-kept part of her was the sleek hair wound up in tight golden braids. Already the bloomy flush of life was gone from this woman and yet there was in her eyes a look that was for old happy, far-off things.

"How was it you happened to have an umbrella when all day it's been sunny?" she asked me suspiciously. She pulled Mary inside, with her three other children.

"I'm the summer preacher at the cross-ways church," I explained, smiling: "At prayer-meeting the other night we asked God for rain. So I thought I had better pack an umbrella."

Her gaze was pitying. Motioning me inside, she fastened the door and began peeling off Mary's soaked clothing. On the wall, I was noticing three faded photographs of the same man, a boxer in trunks, balled fists lifted in a John L. Sullivan guard.

"Who's the fighter?" I asked.

From all four children came a shrill chorus: "That's Pop!"

"He used to be light heavy-weight champ!" screamed the older boy.

"He still packs a terrific right!" yelled the other.

"Pop's strong!" said Mary softly.

As the mother hushed her gossipy brood, I changed the subject:—

"You might as well understand," the mother announced stiffly, "that your congregation don't want us. And we sure don't want them. No, there's no mistake. They all think my husband is no good. As long as I stick to Frank, they won't help us. So—"

There was a sudden violent blast of wind as the door was flung open and a man stamped in; a dripping wreck but still recognizable as the boxer on the walls.

"You that summer Reverend?" he demanded.

"Yes—I'm John Bonnell,—"

The light heavy-weight pointed with backward thumb toward the stormy outdoors; I had to wave good-bye to his silent wife and children, and ride off.

It was, therefore, a prodigious shock to me, at the Sunday service to behold Frank Sanders, scrubbed and shaved sitting all by himself in the back pew. Why had the dilapidated slugger come to church?

Since Sanders had turned me out of his house, I had been making inquiries. Emily, his wife, as laundress and spare helper, earned the family money, while he hunted rabbits and wild geese, and fished in the ponds. A lot of his time was spent with his lone friend, whom everybody called Doctor Tom. This broken-down professor kept Frank in whiskey, and sent him on errands, fetching newspapers and mail to a reeking bachelor cabin on the other side of town. I had good reason to wonder about the business of the atheist's apprentice in my congregation.

After the service, Frank remained stolidly in his pew, until all the other parishioners were waiting outside by the graveyard gate; they thought I was facing a fight.

"Mr. Sanders," I told him, "you're welcome here."

"Don't get any ideas, Reverend," he reported, rising with a wink. "I don't believe in pious balderdash."

"Is that boxing lingo?" I asked. "Sounds more like your friend, Doctor Tom. Frank, why did you come?"

"Reverend, you want to attract crowds to your meetings, don't you? Well, you're going to get 'em. Because I'm going to be here every time you have a service. That's bound to set people talking. They'll come in droves, hoping for the knockout—want to see me plead to be saved from my sins. Hah! You realize I'm never going to do any such thing!"

"Then why," I demanded, quite bewildered, "do you want me to have crowds?"

"For the nice help you gave our Mary in the rain, Reverend. When I ordered you out of my house I didn't realize—so I've got to square myself."

Chin up and whistling, he walked off, his face toward the hills, and his friend, Doctor Tom. . . .

Never before had our little gray church with the red steeple held such crowds; the splintery pine benches could not seat them all. And Frank, keeping his promise, was invariably there, in the last row, and at first, alone. Later he brought in the whole family, starched, and well behaved. And later still, I learned that he had taken a job in the planing mill; for more than a month he kept sober.

But one morning I was stopped, in front of the general store, by a puffy, red-whiskered man who barred my path and held up a bottle.

"Look, Rev!" he panted. "If I fill this with water, can you change it into good hard liquor?"

Getting no answer from me, he turned to Frank Sanders, just coming out of the store.

"I suppose," he shouted, "he's got you to believe in the miracle of changing water into wine!"

"Doctor Tom, I can tell you a bigger miracle than that," Frank grinned. "He's turned rum into food and clothing right in my now happy home."

"Balderdash!" tittered Doctor Tom amiably, holding on to my lapel. "Listen, Rev! Suppose you think you're converting Frank. Well let me prophesy what's going to happen, immediately after you go back where you came from. Good old Frank will quit his job. Immediately! He'll junk his family. Immediately! And he'll come back to me! Immediately!"

"And you consider that a good thing?"

"At least he can have a little fun for himself out of this so-called life. You won't get him. I'll get him. You'll see."

Off he waddled, toward the hill road, but over his shoulder, he called back:

"Ask Frank what he'll be doing next Christmas Eve."

There was deep worry in Frank's eyes.

"Whether I can stick it out after you've gone back to school, Reverend, I just ain't sure. This is a lot tougher fight for me than you might realize. What keeps me going, is listening to you— you're like my trainer in the corner, my second; you keep up my nerve. Everybody needs somebody in his corner."

"Everybody has Somebody," I told him. "You can count on Him, too."

He flashed me a blank look of doubt.

"You can't see Him though," he muttered. "He ain't got skin on. I won't be able to see Him next Christmas Eve."

That was the crux of his fear. For the last five years Frank had gone into Earlton with money for Christmas toys and then drunk himself into a stupor.

"That's what Doctor Tom is counting on now," he finished miserably.

"Frank," I said impulsively, "if you can keep going steady right up to the morning of December 24, I'll come back up here to see you through Christmas Eve."

"Reverend," cried my friend, "that's a deal!"

After the first week in September, when I went back to Halifax, the church at Renshaw was shut up until spring. A letter from Emily Sanders told me how Frank was sticking to his job and even talking about building some fine new pews for the church. But the hardwood he wanted was scarce, except for a big stock in Doctor Tom's back yard, and the professor refused to sell unless Frank Sanders would take a drink with him.

"So far," wrote Emily, "Frank hasn't taken it, but he will do almost anything for the church now."

Doesn't it seem strange that by the time the holidays came around, I had forgotten my Christmas Eve appointment? I don't know why I did, except that school work had been completely absorbing all that autumn, and now my folks were planning a jolly time over the fortnight; had even invited as their house-guest a young woman in whom I had become deeply interested. I was even considering a romantic Christmas morning proposal beside the yule tree. What reminded me, just in time, was a run-through of my diary; I was making notes for Christmas greetings and suddenly came upon the name of Frank Sanders.

By telephone calls, I made my excuses, and grabbed the first train for the Grand Pre' country. At noon I was once more at the Sanders house in Renshaw, but I was too late.

"Frank's gone to the county seat with all the other men," Emily told me. "He took the money for the toys. But when you didn't arrive on the morning train, the heart seemed to go right out of him."

"I'll drive after him," I exclaimed. "I'll hire an automobile."

But in those innocent days, Renshaw had no cars for hire. I was marooned in town.

That night, when the return train from town was due, I stood with Emily on the platform. What would we see when the train arrived; Frank Sanders drunk or sober? We were afraid to look at each other; afraid of the answers already in our eyes. Presently, in fur-cap and jacket, and smoking a cigar, Doctor Tom accosted us.

"Well!" he exclaimed, with a snort that would have done credit to a bull-moose. Raising his voice, so that everyone could hear, he added:—"What are you keeping this poor woman waiting here for? Emily Sanders knows as well as I do what's coming home to her on that train. Immediately!"

"Pray, Reverend," murmured Emily. "The train ride home is the worst part. Everybody has a bottle to pass around. Pray hard!"

"Pray, hah! That *shows* you're not sure. Well, I'm sure! Enough to bet good hard cash! Who'll take me up? Who has five bucks that says Frankie Sanders gets off that train sober—who? What! Nobody? Three dollars? Two, then. Surely for two measly bucks somebody in this crowd will bet on good old Frank. Think, neighbors—you're betting on a human soul. So the parson says! How about you, Rev? Will you bet a buck?''

"Don't believe in gambling," I told him.

"You mean you don't believe in Frank Sanders—not even a buck's worth!''

Was it righteous wrath or just plain temper? To this day I am not sure. Then as now, I detested gambling. Yet I said:

"I'll take your bet. If Frank Sanders come home a sober man, you will give the hardwood stored in your back shed to be made into new pews for the church. Otherwise, I pay you the price of the wood.''

"It's a bet?''

"It is,'' I concurred shakily, "a bet!''

No one would ever have expected Doctor Tom and myself to shake hands. Yet we did, and none too soon, for already on the snowy night we heard the far-off whistle of the train. Shamelessly holding the hand of another man's wife, I prayed to Almighty God that I would win this, my first and last wager. I remember the confusion of my feelings; the torment of soul; in the woofed phantasies of those last waiting minutes it seemed to me that here at this provincial crossroads was all the trouble of the world, the struggle of good and evil making the wind-swept platform an everywhere—and the result very much a doubt.

Now we could hear the bell, loud and strong, and we all stood in the yellow flame of the headlight, gleaming on walls of snow, as the engine, hauling two dim-lit coaches, came snuffling to a stop.

Farmers and breeders and orchard men streamed off the train but there was no sign of Frank. Doctor Tom looked around him with a toothy smile, as I climbed aboard and marched through the cars, peering under seats and in the washrooms, like a woodsman looking for a wounded animal. As I came out on the back steps, I shouted:

"Hasn't anybody seen Frank Sanders?''

The engineer, bending far out the window of the cab, called hoarsely:

"Sure, I seen him. About two hours before train time. He was going into the Blue Nose Tavern.''

That was all we needed to know. There was an audible sigh from the crowd as they turned and surged on toward the bridge over the tracks. As I took Emily by the arm and we started off together, I came as near to weeping as is good for a senior student. How I hated myself for not anticipating. Why hadn't I brought toys myself, to make sure?

Beyond the bridge loomed a wagon, drawn by two white horses. The driver stood up and waved his hat:

"Merry Christmas, everybody!"

And then suddenly I saw—and all the others saw with me,—a familiar figure clambering from behind the load of barrels and casks. It was Frank Sanders jumping to the snow-packed highway, and the driver was handing down to him a doll and a drum, a ship and a toy cradle, a whole Santa Claus cargo of Christmas toys.

"Hey, Emily!" Frank was yelling. "Don't get scared. Ain't had a drop! Thought it was safer not to come home on the train. Too much temptation, with bottles being passed and all. So I hopped a ride home on the Blue Tavern's truck."

Emily ran toward him and then for the first time he saw me.

"Rev!" he yelled. "You *did* come! Well, thanks. But you were right. There was Somebody in my corner all the time—even among the beer kegs! Knowing that fixes everything. Come on home and help trim the tree."

"First," I told him, "I've got to see Doctor Tom—and make sure the church collects my winnings. Immediately!"

Then, behind banker George Mason's back
the huge door swung shut. He was locked in the vault.

The Man Who Missed Christmas
by J. Edgar Parks*

On Christmas Eve, as usual, George Mason was the last to leave
the office. He stood for a moment at the window, watching the
hurrying crowds below, the strings of colored Christmas lights,
the fat Santa Clauses on the street corners. He was a slender man
in his late thirties, this George Mason, not conspicuously successful or brilliant, but a good executive— he ran his office
efficiently and well.

Abruptly he turned and walked over to a massive safe set into
the far wall. He spun the dials, swung the heavy door open. A
light went on, revealing a vault of polished steel as large as a
small room. George Mason carefully propped a chair against the
open door of the safe and stepped inside.

He took three steps forward, tilting his head so that he could
see the square of white cardboard taped just above the topmost
row of strongboxes. On the card a few words were written.
George Mason stared at those words, remembering. . . .

Exactly one year ago he had entered this selfsame vault. He
had planned a rather expensive, if solitary, evening; had decided
he might need a little additional cash. He had not bothered to
prop the door; ordinarily friction held the balanced mass of metal
in place. But only that morning the people who serviced the safe
had cleaned and oiled it. And then, behind George Mason's
back, slowly, noiselessly, the ponderous door swung shut. There
was a click of springlocks. The automatic light went out, and he
was trapped—entombed in the sudden and terrifying dark.

Instantly, panic seized him. He hurled himself at the unyield-
ing door. He gave a hoarse cry; the sound was like an explosion
in that confined place. In the silence that followed, he heard the

*Adapted by Arthur Gordon

frantic thudding of his heart. Through his mind flashed all the stories he had heard of men found suffocated in timevaults. No timeclock controlled this mechanism; the safe would remain locked until it was opened from the outside. Tomorrow morning.

Then the sickening realization struck him. No one would come tomorrow morning—tomorrow was Christmas Day.

Once more he flung himself at the door, shouting wildly, beating with his hands until he sank on his knees exhausted. Silence again, highpitched, singing silence that seemed deafening.

George Mason was no smoker; he did not carry matches. Except for the tiny luminous dial of his watch, the darkness was absolute. The blackness almost had texture: it was tangible, stifling. The time now was 6:15. More than 36 hours would pass before anyone entered the office. Thirty-six hours in a steel box three feet wide, eight feet long, seven feet high. Would the oxygen last, or would . . .

Like a flash of lightning a memory came to him, dim with the passage of time. What had they told him when they installed the safe? Something about a safety measure for just such a crisis as this.

Breathing heavily, he felt his way around the floor. The palms of his hands were sweating. But in the far righthand corner, just above the floor, he found it: a small, circular opening some two inches in diameter. He thrust his finger into it and felt, faint but mistakable, a cool current of air.

The tension release was so sudden that he burst into tears. But at last he sat up. Surely he would not have to stay trapped for the full 36 hours. Somebody would miss him, would make inquiries, would come to release him. . . .

But who? He was unmarried and lived alone. The maid who cleaned his apartment was just a servant; he had always treated her as such. He had been invited to spend Christmas Eve with his brother's family, but children got on his nerves, and expected presents.

A friend had asked him to go to a home for elderly people on Christmas Day and play the piano—George Mason was a good musician. But he had made some excuse or other; he had intended to sit at home with a good cigar, listening to some new recordings he was giving himself for Christmas.

George Mason dug his nails into the palms of his hands until the pain balanced the misery in his mind. He had thrown away his chances. Nobody would come and let him out. Nobody, nobody . . .

Marked by the luminous hands of the watch, the leaden-footed seconds ticked away. He slept a little, but not much. He felt no hunger, but he was tormented by thirst. Miserably the whole of Christmas Day went by, and the succeeding night. . . .

On the morning after Christmas the head clerk came into the office at the usual time. He opened the safe but did not bother to swing the heavy door wide. Then he went on into his private office.

No one saw George Mason stagger out into the corridor, run to the water cooler, and drink great gulps of water. No one paid any attention to him as he descended to the street and took a taxi home.

There he shaved, changed his wrinkled clothes, ate some breakfast and returned to his office, where his employees greeted him pleasantly but casually.

On his way to lunch that day he met several acquaintances, but not a single one had noticed his Christmas absence. He even met his own brother, who was a member of the same luncheon club, but his brother failed to ask if he had enjoyed Christmas.

Grimly, inexorably, the truth closed in on George Mason. He had vanished from human society during the great festival of brotherhood and fellowship, and no one had missed him at all.

Reluctantly, almost with a sense of dread, George Mason began to think about the true meaning of Christmas. Was it possible that he had been blind all these years, blind with selfishness, with indifference, with pride? Wasn't Christmas the time when men went out of their way to share with one another the joy of Christ's birth? Wasn't giving, after all, the essence of Christmas because it marked the time God gave His own Son to the world?

All through the year that followed, with little hesitant deeds of kindness, with small, unnoticed acts of unselfishness, George Mason tried to prepare himself. . . .

Now, once more, it was Christmas Eve.

Slowly he backed out of the safe, closed it. He touched its grim steel face lightly, almost affectionately, as if it were an old friend. He picked up his hat and coat, and certain bundles. Then he left the office, descended to the busy street.

There he goes now in his black overcoat and hat, the same George Mason as a year ago. Or is it? He walks a few blocks, then flags a taxi, anxious not to be late. His nephews are expecting him to help them trim the tree. Afterwards, he is taking his brother and his sister-in-law to a Christmas play. Why is he so inexpressibly happy? Why does this jostling against others, laden as he is with bundles, exhilarate and delight him?

Perhaps the card has something to do with it, the card he taped inside his office safe last New Year's Day. On the card is written, in George Mason's own hand: *To love people, to be indispensable somewhere, that is the purpose of life. That is the secret of happiness.*

A legend yes, but full of faith.

The Miraculous Staircase
by Arthur Gordon

On that cool December morning in 1878, sunlight lay like an amber rug across the dusty streets and adobe houses of Santa Fe. It glinted on the bright tile roof of the almost completed Chapel of Our Lady of Light and on the nearby windows of the convent school run by the Sisters of Loretto. Inside the convent, the Mother Superior looked up from her packing as a tap came on her door.

"It's *another* carpenter, Reverend Mother," said Sister Francis Louise, her round face apologetic. "I told him that you're leaving right away, that you haven't time to see him, but he says . . ."

"I know what he says," Mother Magdalene said, going on resolutely with her packing. "That he's heard about our problem with the new chapel. That he's the best carpenter in all of New Mexico. That he can build us a staircase to the choir loft despite the fact that the brilliant architect in Paris who drew the plans failed to leave any space for one. And despite the fact that five master carpenters have already tried and failed. You're quite right, Sister; I don't have time to listen to that story again."

"But he seems such a nice man," said Sister Francis Louise wistfully, "and he's out there with his burro, and . . . ."

"I'm sure," said Mother Magdalene with a smile, "that he's a charming man, and that his burro is a charming donkey. But there's sickness down at the Santo Domingo pueblo, and it may be cholera. Sister Mary Helen and I are the only ones here who've had cholera. So we have to go. And you have to stay and run the school. And that's that!" Then she called, "Manuela!"

A young Indian girl of 12 or 13, black-haired and smiling, came in quietly on moccasined feet. She was a mute. She could hear and understand, but the Sisters had been unable to teach her to speak. The Mother Superior spoke to her gently: "Take my things down to the wagon, child. I'll be right there." And to Sister Francis Louise: "You'd better tell your carpenter friend to come back in two or three weeks. I'll see him then."

"Two or three weeks! Surely you'll be home for Christmas?"

"If it's the Lord's will, Sister. I hope so."

In the street, beyond the waiting wagon, Mother Magdalene could see the carpenter, a bearded man, strongly built and taller than most Mexicans, with dark eyes and a smiling, wind-burned face. Beside him, laden with tools and scraps of lumber, a small gray burro stood patiently. Manuela was stroking its nose, glancing shyly at its owner. "You'd better explain," said the Mother Superior, "that the child can hear him, but she can't speak."

Goodbyes were quick—the best kind when you leave a place you love. Southwest, then, along the dusty trail, the mountains purple with shadow, the Rio Grande a ribbon of green far off to the right. The pace was slow, but Mother Magdalene and Sister Mary Helen amused themselves by singing songs and telling Christmas stories as the sun marched up and down the sky. And their leathery driver listened and nodded.

Two days of this brought them to Santo Domingo Pueblo, where the sickness was not cholera after all, but measles, almost as deadly in an Indian village. And so they stayed, helping the harassed Father Sebastian, visitng the dark adobe hovels where feverish brown children tossed and fierce Indian dogs showed their teeth.

At night they were boneweary, but sometimes Mother Magdalene found time to talk to Father Sebastian about her plans for the dedication of the new chapel. It was to be in April; the Archbishop himself would be there. And it might have been dedicated sooner, were it not for this incredible business of a choir loft with no means of access—unless it were a ladder.

"I told the Bishop," said Mother Magdalene, "that it would be a mistake to have the plans drawn in Paris. If something went wrong, what could we do? But he wanted our chapel in Santa Fe patterned after the Sainte Chapelle in Paris, and who am I to argue with Bishop Lamy? So the talented Monsieur Mouly designs a beautiful choir loft high up under the rose window, and no way to get up to it."

"Perhaps," sighed Father Sebastian, "he had in mind a heavenly choir. The kind with wings."

"It's not funny," said Mother Magdalene a bit sharply. "I've prayed and prayed, but apparently there's no solution at all. There just isn't room on the chapel floor for the supports such a staircase needs."

The days passed, and with each passing day Christmas drew closer. Twice, horsemen on their way from Santa Fe to Albuquerque brought letters from Sister Francis Louise. All was well at the convent, but Mother Magdalene frowned over certain paragraphs. "The children are getting ready for Christmas," Sister Francis Louise wrote in her first letter. "Our little Manuela and the carpenter have become great friends. It's amazing how much he seems to know about us all. . . ."

And what, thought Mother Magdalene, is the carpenter still doing there?

The second letter also mentioned the carpenter. "Early every morning he comes with another load of lumber, and every night he goes away. When we ask him by what authority he does these things, he smiles and says nothing. We have tried to pay him for his work, but he will accept no pay . . ."

Work? What work? Mother Magdalene wrinkled up her nose in exasperation. Had that softhearted Sister Francis Louise given the man permission to putter around in the new chapel? With firm and disapproving hand the Mother Superior wrote a note ordering an end to all such unauthorized activities. She gave it to an Indian potterymaker on his way to Santa Fe.

But that night the first snow fell, so thick and heavy that the Indian turned back. Next day at noon the sun shone again on a world glittering with diamonds. But Mother Magdalene knew that another snowfall might make it impossible for her to be home for Christmas. By now the sickness at Santo Domingo was subsiding. And so that afternoon they began the long ride back.

The snow did come again, making their slow progress even slower. It was late on Christmas Eve, close to midnight, when the tired horses plodded up to the convent door. But lamps still burned. Manuela flew down the steps, Sister Francis Louise close behind her. And chilled and weary though she was, Mother Magdalene sensed instantly an excitement, an electricity in the air that she could not understand.

Nor did she understand it when they led her, still in her heavy wraps, down the corridor, into the new, as-yet-unused chapel where a few candles burned. "Look Reverend Mother," breathed Sister Francis Louise. "Look!"

Like a curl of smoke the staircase rose before them, as insubstantial as a dream. Its base was on the chapel floor; its top rested against the choir loft. Nothing else supported it; it seemed to float on air. There were no banisters. Two complete spirals it made, the polished wood gleaming softly in the candlelight. "Thirty-three steps," whispered Sister Francis Louise. "One for each year in the life of Our Lord."

Mother Magdalene moved forward like a woman in a trance. She put her foot on the first step, then the second, then the third. There was not a tremor. She looked down, bewildered, at Manuela's ecstatic, upturned face. "But it's impossible! There wasn't time!"

"He finished yesterday," the Sister said. "He didn't come today. No one has seen him anywhere in Santa Fe. He's gone."

"But *who* was he? Don't you even know his *name?*"

The Sister shook her head, but now Manuela pushed forward, nodding emphatically. Her mouth opened; she took a deep, shuddering breath; she made a sound that was like a gasp in the stillness. The nuns stared at her, transfixed. She tried again. This time it was a syllable, followed by another. "Jo-sé." She clutched the Mother Superior's arm and repeated the first word she had ever spoken. "José!"

Sister Francis Louise crossed herself. Mother Magdalene felt her heart contract. José—the Spanish word for Joseph. Joseph the Carpenter. Joseph the Master Woodworker of . . .

"José!" Manuela's dark eyes were full of tears. "José!"

Silence, then, in the shadowy chapel. No one moved. Far away across the snow-silvered town Mother Magdalene heard a bell tolling midnight. She came down the stairs and took Manuela's hand. She felt uplifted by a great surge of wonder and gratitude and compassion and love. And she knew what it was. It was the spirit of Christmas. And it was upon them all.

Author's Note: The wonderful thing about legends is the way they grow. Through the years they can be told and retold and embroidered a bit more each time. This, indeed, is such a retelling. But all good legends contain a grain of truth, and in this case the irrefutable fact at the heart of the legend is the inexplicable staircase itself.

You may see it yourself in Santa Fe today. It stands just as it stood when the chapel was dedicated almost 90 years ago—except for the banister, which was added later.

Tourists stare and marvel. Architects shake their heads and murmur, "Impossible." No one knows the identity of the designer-builder. All the Sisters know is that the problem existed, a stranger came, solved it and left.

The 33 steps make two complete turns without central support. There are no nails in the staircase; only wooden pegs. The curved stringers are put together with exquisite precision; the wood is spliced in seven places on the inside and nine on the outside. The wood is said to be a hard-fir variety, nonexistent in New Mexico. School records show that no payment for the staircase was ever made.

Who is real and who is imaginary in this version of the story? Mother Mary Magdalene was indeed the first Mother Superior; she came to Santa Fe by riverboat and covered wagon in 1852. Bishop J. B. Lamy was indeed her Bishop. And Monsieur Projectus Mouly of Paris was indeed the absent-minded architect.

Sister Francis Louise? Well, there must have been someone like her. And Manuela, the Indian girl, came out of nowhere to help with the embroidery.

The carpenter himself? Ah, who can say?

It was not the first time a son had
made that hard trip home.

The Runaway Boy
by Chase Walker

There is something about a holiday that turns normally silent
people—total strangers—into secret-confiding friends.

Such was the case one Christmas Eve not long ago aboard a
speeding Midwestern train. The electric spirit of the season
seemed to fill each car. In one seat, a little girl, sporting a big
yellow bow in her hair, asked anxiously, "How much longer to
Grandma's?"

A few seats away, a sailor proudly held out a wallet-sized
photograph of his sweetheart, showing it to the others around
him.

Everyone seemed to be talking and laughing. Everyone except
one young man and his seat companion, a kindly looking
gentleman with gray-white hair. The man had vainly attempted
to start a conversation, but the boy was preoccupied. He never
looked away from the window.

Finally, the man gave up and went back to reading his
book—until he realized the young man was crying, a muffled,
quiet crying, but unmistakably crying.

"Need a handkerchief?" the man asked.

"Yes, sir," answered the boy. "Thank you."

There was a moment's silence.

"Is there anything I can do, Son?"

"No, I'm afraid not. It's too late. . . ." The boy put the
handkerchief to his face again.

Placing his hand on the boy's shoulder, the man consoled him,
"Sometimes we only think it's too late. Why don't you tell me
the problem. Let me decide."

"Well . . ." the boy hesitated, then began:

"It was four months ago . . . well, almost four months. You
see, I ran away from home. I just couldn't take it anymore . . . my

school work was horrible . . . and I was sick to death of doing chores morning and night. Well, I told Dad and we had a terrible argument. That night I packed some clothes and headed for the city. I had a little money saved and figured I could get a job. In less than a week I realized that I had made a mistake. I was tempted to tell Mom and Dad that I wanted to come home when I wrote them not to worry, but I was too embarrassed. Many nights I slept in the streets, hungry more often than not."

The boy blew his nose and dabbed at his eyes again. "Finally, last week I broke down and wrote Dad that I wanted to come home, though I knew he might not want me back. I told him I'd be on this train, and that if I was welcome he should tie a red cloth on the big elm at the back of the farm. The train runs right past our farm and that old tree drapes over the fence."

"Well, I think you'll be welcome, Son," the man assured him. Picking up the book which had lain in his lap, the old man leafed through it. "You probably think your story is unique, but in this book, this Bible, there is a story much like yours. It's the story of the Prodigal Son. Do you know it?"

The boy shook his head no.

"Then I want to read it to you." And the old man read that familiar story. When he had finished, the boy's face wore a smile.

"I believe most fathers are filled with the same forgiving spirit as in this story," the man said, "and I believe your father will be more than willing to have you back."

The boy suddenly sat upright. "We're almost there," he said. "Our place is right after the next bend. Oh, I'm afraid to look."

"Then I'll look for you," volunteered the man.

The telephone poles raced by. For a moment the man's faith wavered. What if there were no signal in the elm tree?

Just then the train swung around the bend and up ahead he saw the huge elm dancing in the wind, its branches bare against the steel-gray sky and snowy fields. Bare—except for dozens of red banners that flapped from every conceivable limb. They shouted the news to a runaway boy that all was forgiven at Christmas.

Georgie Potter kept his promise.

The Kidnapping in Victory Church

It was Christmas morning, 1933, that the Pastor of Our Lady of Victory Church in San Francisco was interrupted at his morning prayers. His sexton was in such turmoil he could barely speak, and behind him the young Curate was pale and wide-eyed.

"I've just opened the church, Father, and found the Infant, Father—the Christ Child is gone! Gone from the manger-crib!"

"That's absurd!" The old priest rose to his feet as he looked disbelievingly from one to the other. He strode with some exasperation down the rectory stairs and into the church. The first Mass of the day, at 6 that morning, was barely a half hour away. What kind of panic would sweep through the parish when the people found the Christ Child gone?

Even before he had verified the disappearance for himself, the priest's thoughts were concerned with the thief. What kind of fiend—what infidel—would so outrage a shrine? Was this perpetrated by someone who wished to defile and desecrate the symbol of the very birth of Christianity? Or was it for revenge on the priest, the congregation, or upon God and his Church?

"Shall we call the police, father?" the Curate asked.

The old priest shook his head. He glanced about the church he loved and which only four and a half hours ago had been filled with the happiest crowds of the year, the attenders of Midnight Mass. He wanted no scandal to touch his church. He walked away silently.

Back in the rectory he got into his overcoat and rubbers. The streets were clean with snow. Already the early crowd was coming to church, and he greeted those he passed with a hearty "Merry Christmas" he did not feel. As he reached a corner, a small boy, running as he pulled an express wagon, almost knocked him down.

257

"Georgie Potter!" the priest began, indignantly, but at the sight of the upturned ruddy shining little face of the seven-year-old, he sighed and smiled. "Now, is that a new wagon I see?"

"Yes, Father!"

"You're up early enough to get your presents, I must say." Suddenly the priest stiffened. *"Georgie! What-is-that-in-your wagon?"*

The Christ Child! The priest stared transfixed. The beloved statuette of the Infant Jesus with its baby arms outstretched in wide benediction lay with a blanket tucked about it!

The shining light was gone from the child's face and he cowered.

"Georgie—did you take that from the church?"

"But I *promised,* Father!" the boy blurted defensively. "I prayed and prayed for a red wagon. And I promised the Christ Child if He'd get me a red wagon for Christmas, I'd give him a ride in it twice 'round the block."

She paid the most anyone can pay for...

A String of Blue Beads
by Fulton Oursler

Pete Richards was the loneliest man in town on the day Jean Grace opened the door to his shop. Pete's small business had come down to him from his grandfather. The little front window was strewn with a disarray of old-fashioned things: bracelets and lockets worn in days before the Civil War, gold rings and silver boxes, images of jade and ivory, porcelain figurines.

On this winter's afternoon a child was standing there, her forehead against the glass, earnest and enormous eyes studying each discarded treasure as if she were looking for something quite special. Finally she straightened up with a satisfied air and entered the store.

The shadowy interior of Pete Richards' establishment was even more cluttered than his show window. Shelves were stacked with jewel caskets, dueling pistols, clocks and lamps, and the floor was heaped with andirons and mandolins and things hard to find a name for.

Behind the counter stood Pete himself, a man not more than 30, but with hair already turning gray. There was a bleak air about him as he looked at the small customer who flattened her ungloved hands on the counter.

"Mister," she began, "would you please let me look at that string of blue beads in the window?"

Pete parted the draperies and lifted out a necklace. The turquoise stones gleamed brightly against the pallor of his palm as he spread the ornament before her.

"They're just perfect," said the child, entirely to herself. "Will you wrap them up pretty for me, please?"

Pete studied her with a stony air. "Are you buying these for someone?"

"They're for my big sister. She takes care of me. You see,

259

this will be the first Christmas since Mother died. I've been looking for the most wonderful Christmas present for my sister."

"How much money do you have?" asked Pete warily.

She had been busily untying the knots in a handkerchief, and now she poured out a handful of pennies on the counter.

"I emptied my bank," she explained simply.

Pete Richards looked at her thoughtfully. Then he carefully drew back the necklace; the price tag was visible to him but not to her. How could he tell her? The trusting look of her blue eyes smote him like the pain of an old wound.

"Just a minute," he said, and turned toward the back of the store. Over his shoulder he called, "What's your name?" He was very busy about something.

"Jean Grace."

When Pete returned to where Jean Grace waited, a package lay in his hand, wrapped in scarlet paper and tied with a bow of green ribbon. "There you are," he said shortly. "Don't lose it on the way home."

She smiled happily at him over her shoulder as she ran out the door. Through the window he watched her go, while desolation flooded his thoughts. Something about Jean Grace and her string of beads had stirred him to the depths of a grief that would not stay buried. The child's hair was wheat yellow, her eyes sea blue, and once upon a time, not long before, Pete had been in love with a girl with hair of that same yellow and with eyes just as blue. And the turquoise necklace was to have been hers.

But there had come a rainy night—a truck skidding on a slippery road—and the life was crushed out of his dream.

Since then Pete Richards had lived too much with his grief in solitude. He was politely attentive to customers, but after business hours his world seemed irrevocably empty.

The blue eyes of Jean Grace jolted him into acute remembrance of what he had lost. The pain of it made him recoil from the exuberance of holiday shoppers. During the next ten days trade was brisk; chattering women swarmed in, fingering trinkets, trying to bargain. When the last customer had gone, late on Christmas Eve, he sighed with relief. It was over for another year. But for Pete Richards the night was not quite over.

The door opened and a young woman hurried in. With an inexplicable start, he realized that she looked familiar, yet he could not remember when or where he had seen her before. Her hair was golden yellow and her large eyes were blue. Without speaking, she drew from her purse a package loosely unwrapped in its red paper, a bow of green ribbon with it. Presently the string of blue beads lay gleaming again before him.

"Did this come from your shop?" she asked.

Pete raised his eyes to hers and answered softly, "Yes, it did."

"Are the stones real?"

"Yes. Not the finest quality—but real."

"Can you remember who it was you sold them to?"

"She was a small girl. Her name was Jean. She bought them for her older sister's Christmas present."

"How much are they worth?"

"The price," he told her solemnly, "is always a confidential matter between the seller and the customer."

"But Jean has never had more than a few pennies of spending money. How could she pay for them?"

Pete was folding the gay paper back into its creases, rewrapping the little package just as neatly as before.

"She paid the biggest price anyone can ever pay," he said. "She gave all she had."

There was a silence then that filled the little curio shop. In some faraway steeple, a bell began to ring. The sound of the distant chiming, the little package lying on the counter, the question in the eyes of the girl and the strange feeling of renewal struggling unreasonably in the heart of the man, all had come to be because of the love of a child.

"But why did you do it?"

He held out the gift in his hand.

"It's already Christmas morning," he said, "and it's my misfortune that I have no one to give anything to. Will you let me see you home and wish you a Merry Christmas at your door?"

And so, to the sound of many bells, and in the midst of happy people, Pete Richards and a girl whose name he had yet to learn walked out into the beginning of the great day that brings hope into the world for us all.

A NEW YEAR's PRAYER

Dear Lord, please give me . . .
A few friends who understand me and yet remain my friends
A work to do which has real value, without which
the world would feel the poorer . . .
A mind unafraid to travel, even though the trail be not
blazed
An understanding heart . . .
A sense of humor.
Time for quiet, silent meditation.
A feeling of the presence of God.
And the patience to wait for the coming of these things,
with the wisdom to know them when they come.

W. R. Hunt

None of the gifts caused the long-silent
bells to stir . . .

The Night the Chimes Rang
by Raymond Macdonald Alden

Once, long ago, a magnificent church stood on a high hill in a great city. When lighted up for a special festival, it could be seen for miles around. And yet there was something even more remarkable about this church than its beauty—the strange and wonderful legend of the bells.

At one corner of the church was a tall gray tower, and at the top of the tower—so people said—was a chime of the most beautiful bells in the world. But the fact was that no one had heard the bells for many years. Not even on Christmas. For it was the custom on Christmas Eve for all the people to bring to the church their offerings to the Christ-child. And there had been a time when a very unusual offering laid on the altar brought glorious music from the chimes far up in the tower. Some said that the wind rang them, and others that the angels set them swinging. But lately no offering had been great enough to deserve the music of the chimes.

Now a few miles from the city, in a small village, lived a boy named Pedro, and his little brother. They knew very little about the Christmas chimes, but they had heard of the service in the church on Christmas Eve, and they decided to go to see the beautiful celebration.

The day before Christmas was bitterly cold, with a hard white crust on the ground. Pedro and Little Brother started out early in the afternoon, and despite the cold they reached the edge of the city by nightfall. They were about to enter one of the great gates when Pedro saw something dark on the snow near their path.

It was a poor woman, who had fallen just outside the city, too sick and tired to get in where she might have found shelter. Pedro tried to rouse her, but she was barely conscious. "It's no use, Little Brother. You will have to go alone."

"Without you?" cried Little Brother.

Pedro nodded slowly. "This poor woman will freeze to death if nobody cares for her. Everyone has probably gone to the church now, but when you come back be sure and bring someone to help her. I will stay here and try to keep her from freezing, and perhaps get her to eat the roll I have in my pocket."

"But I can't leave you!" cried Little Brother.

"Both of us need not miss the service," said Pedro. "You must see and hear everything twice, Little Brother—once for you and once for me. I am sure the Christ-child knows how I would love to worship Him. And if you get a chance, Little Brother, take this silver piece of mine and, when no one is looking, lay it down for my offering."

In this way he hurried Little Brother off to the city, and winked hard to keep back the tears of disappointment.

The great church was a brilliant place that night; it had never looked so beautiful before. When the organ played and the thousands of people sang, the walls shook with the sound.

At the close of the service came the procession with the offerings to be laid on the altar. Some brought wonderful jewels, some heavy baskets of gold. A famous writer laid down a book which he had been writing for years. And last of all walked the king of the country, hoping with all the rest to win for himself the chime of the Christmas bells.

A great murmur went through the church as the king took from his head the royal crown, all set with precious stones, and laid it on the altar. "Surely," everyone said, "we shall hear the bells now!"

But only the cold wind was heard in the tower.

The procession was over, and the choir began the closing hymn. Suddenly the organist stopped playing. The singing ceased. Not a sound could be heard from anyone in the church. As all the people strained their ears to listen, there came—softly, but distinctly—the sound of the chimes in the tower. So far away and yet so clear, the music seemed so much sweeter than anything ever heard before.

Then they all stood up together and looked at the altar to see what great gift had awakened the long-silent bells. But all they saw was the childish figure of Little Brother, who had crept softly down the aisle when no one was looking and had laid Pedro's little piece of silver on the altar.

Season's Greetings

by Fra Giovanni

I am your friend, and my love for you goes deep.
    There is nothing I can give you which you have not got;
But there is much, very much, that, while I cannot give it,
    You can take.
No heaven can come to us unless our hearts
    Find rest in today. Take Heaven!
No peace lies in the future which is not hidden
    In this present little instant. Take Peace!
The gloom of the world is but a shadow.
    Behind it, yet within our reach, is Joy.
There is radiance and glory in the darkness,
    Could we but see, and to see, we have only to look.
I beseech you to look.
Life is so generous a giver, but we,
    Judging its gifts by their covering,
Cast them away as ugly, or heavy, or hard.
    Remove the covering, and you will find beneath it
A living splendor, woven of love, by wisdom, with power.
Welcome it, grasp it, and you touch the
    Angel's hand that brings it to you.
Everything we call a trial, a sorrow, or a duty,
    Believe me, that Angel's hand is there; the gift is there,
And the wonder of an overshadowing Presence.
    Our joys too: be not content with them as joys.
They, too, conceal Diviner gifts.
Life is so full of meaning and purpose.
    So full of Beauty—beneath its covering—
That you will find earth but cloaks your heaven.
Courage then to claim it: that is all!
    But courage you have; and the knowledge that we

Are pilgrims together,
    Wending through unknown country, home.
And so, at this time, I greet you.
    Not quite as the world sends greetings,
But with profound esteem and with the prayer
    That for you now and forever,
The day breaks, and the shadows flee away.

It would have been much different...

≈

If He Had Not Come
by Norman Vincent Peale

*There are many Christmas stories whose warmth and wonder
touch our hearts. This is one I used to tell my children when they
were small because, simple though it is, it reminds us all of
something we sometimes tend to forget: the importance of keeping Christ in Christmas . . .*

It was Christmas Eve—the one night in the year when 7-year-
old Bobby was in a hurry to go to bed. His stocking was tacked
to the mantel; the beautiful tree stood in the corner. He kissed his
mother and father good-night. Then he raced upstairs and leaped
into bed.

It seemed to Bobby that he hadn't been asleep any time when
a harsh voice shouted, "Get up!" He opened his eyes, blinking
in the bright sunlight. Then he remembered what day it was.
With a joyful shout he hurried into his clothes and bounded down
the stairs.

On the bottom step he stopped. No stocking hung from the
mantel. The Christmas tree was gone too. "But . . . but I put the
paper angels on myself," Bobby began, when the shrill whistle
from the factory nearby made him jump.

"The factory can't be open on Christmas!" Bobby thought, as
he put on his coat and ran out of the house. The gateman at the
factory was his friend. He would tell Bobby why—

"Clear out of here, you!" The gateman jerked his thumb at
him. "No kids allowed!"

As Bobby slowly turned to go, he saw to his amazement that
up and down the street all the stores were open. "Why are they
open on Christmas?" he asked a woman coming out of the
supermarket.

"Christmas?" the woman asked. "What's that?"

The hardware store, the bakery, the five-and-ten—everywhere

it was the same. People were busy. They were cross. They'd never heard of Christmas.

"I know one place where they've heard of Christmas!" Bobby cried.

"At my church! There's a special service this morning!"

He started to run. Here was the street! At least he thought it was. But here was only a weed-grown vacant lot. The tower with the carillon bells, the Sunday School windows where Bobby had pasted snowflakes—there was nothing here.

Just then, from the tall grass near the side of the road, Bobby heard a moan. A man was lying on the ground.

"A car struck me!" he gasped. "Never even stopped!"

"Help!" called Bobby to a lady walking past. "This man's hurt!"

The lady jerked Bobby away. "Don't touch him! He doesn't live here. We don't know anything about him."

"I'll run to the hospital, mister," Bobby promised. "They'll send an ambulance!" And he tore off down the street.

"Hospital Of The Good Samaritan," Bobby had often read the name over the archway in the great stone wall. But now the stone wall ran around an empty field. Where the name of the hospital had been, was carved instead, *If He Had Not Come*.

Suddenly Bobby was running home as if his life depended on it. Last night his father had read from the Bible! Maybe the Bible would tell him why everything was changed.

The Bible was still lying on the table in the living room. Bobby snatched it up, ran upstairs to his room. But where the New Testament should have started, there were only blank pages. There was no Christmas story—no Jesus at all. Bobby flung himself on his bed and began to cry . . .

"Merry Christmas, Bobby!" It was his mother's voice from downstairs. "Aren't you getting up on Christmas morning?"

Bobby sprang out of bed and ran to the window. There was a Christmas wreath on the house across the street. And suddenly the carillon bells from the church tower began to ring: *Joy to the World! The Lord is Come!*

"Here I come, Mother!" Bobby called. But he paused at the door and shut his eyes.

"You came!" he whispered. "Thank You for coming!"

> Suddenly there was with the angel
> a multitude of the heavenly host...

The Greatest Story Ever Told
by Saint Luke

And Joseph also went up from Galilee, out of the city of Nazareth, into Judaea, unto the city of David, which is called Bethlehem...to be taxed with Mary his espoused wife, being great with child.

And so it was, that, while they were there, the days were accomplished that she should be delivered.

And she brought forth her firstborn Son, and wrapped Him in swaddling clothes, and laid Him in a manger; because there was no room for them in the inn.

And there were in the same country shepherds abiding in the field, keeping watch over their flock by night.

And, lo, the angel of the Lord came upon them, and the glory of the Lord shone round about them: and they were sore afraid.

And the angel said unto them, Fear not: for, behold, I bring you good tidings of great joy, which shall be to all people.

For unto you is born this day in the city of David a Saviour, which is Christ the Lord.

And this shall be a sign unto you; Ye shall find the Babe wrapped in swaddling clothes, lying in a manger.

And suddenly there was with the angel a multitude of the heavenly host praising God, and saying, Glory to God in the highest, and on earth peace, good will toward men.

Heartwarming Books
of
Faith and Inspiration

☐	14725	**PILGRIMS REGRESS** C. S. Lewis	$2.50
☐	20464	**LOVE AND LIVING** Thomas Merton	$3.50
☐	20618	**A SEVERE MERCY** Sheldon Vanauken	$2.95
☐	01184	**HE WAS ONE OF US: THE LIFE OF JESUS OF NAZARETH** Rien Poortvliet	$9.95
☐	14826	**POSITIVE PRAYERS FOR POWER-FILLED LIVING** Robert H. Schuller	$2.25
☐	20133	**REACH OUT FOR A NEW LIFE** Robert H. Schuller	$2.50
☐	14732	**HOW CAN I FIND YOU, GOD?** Marjorie Holmes	$2.50
☐	13588	**IN SEARCH OF HISTORIC JESUS** Lee Roddy & Charles E. Sellier, Jr.	$2.25
☐	13890	**THE FINDING OF JASPER HOLT** Grace Livingston Hill	$1.75
☐	14385	**THE BIBLE AS HISTORY** Werner Keller	$3.50
☐	20613	**THE GREATEST SALESMAN IN THE WORLD** Og Mandino	$2.50
☐	14216	**THE GREATEST SALESMAN IN THE WORLD** Og Mandino	$2.25
☐	14971	**I'VE GOT TO TALK TO SOMEBODY, GOD** Marjorie Holmes	$2.50
☐	12853	**THE GIFT OF INNER HEALING** Ruth Carter Stapleton	$1.95
☐	12444	**BORN AGAIN** Charles Colson	$2.50
☐	14840	**A GRIEF OBSERVED** C. S. Lewis	$2.50
☐	14770	**TWO FROM GALILEE** Marjorie Holmes	$2.50
☐	20727	**LIGHTHOUSE** Eugenia Price	$2.95
☐	14406	**NEW MOON RISING** Eugenia Price	$2.50
☐	20272	**THE LATE GREAT PLANET EARTH** Hal Lindsey	$2.75

Buy them at your local bookstore or use this handy coupon for ordering: